EYEWITNESS

A Study from 1, 2, 3 John

crystal colp • jacki kachner • erin lehmann • alice park

Published by Warner Press
Warner Press and "WP" logo are trademarks of Warner Press
Eyewitness
A Study from the Books of 1, 2, 3 John
Copyright ©2015 by Colp, Kachner, Lehmann, and Park
Cover Art and layout copyright ©2015 by Warner Press Inc

Tree 1:3, an imprint of Warner Press, publishes ministry resources designed to help people grow more deeply in their faith.

The Holy Bible, English Standard Version Copyright © 2001 by Crossway Bibles, a publishing ministry of Good News Publishers.

The Message (MSG) Copyright © 1993, 1994, 1995, 1996, 2000, 2001, 2002 by Eugene H. Peterson.

(NIV) Holy Bible, New International Version®, NIV® Copyright © 1973, 1978, 1984, 2011 by Biblica, Inc.® Used by permission. All rights reserved worldwide.

(NIV1984) - HOLY BIBLE, NEW INTERNATIONAL VERSION®. Copyright © 1973, 1978, 1984 by International Bible Society. Used by permission of Zondervan Publishing House. All rights reserved.

(NLT) New Living Translation copyright © 1996, 2004, 2007 by Tyndale House Foundation. Used by permission of Tyndale House Publishers Inc, Carol Stream, Illinois 60188. All rights reserved.

(NRSV) New Revised Standard Version Bible, copyright © 1989 the Division of Christian Education of the National Council of the Churches of Christ in the United States of America. Used by permission. All rights reserved.

Editors: Karen Rhodes, Robin Fogle
Cover, Design and Layout by Curtis Corzine

ISBN: 978-1-59317-780-5

Printed in the United States of America

Dedicated to
all of the Godly men and women who have
influenced us in our Christian walks.
If we were to list names,
the list would be extensive.
You know who you are,
and we would not be writing Bible studies
without your influence in our lives.
We thank God upon every remembrance of you!

CONTENTS

GREETINGS

Welcome to 1, 2, & 3 John! As I write this, Erin and I both have returning high school Boys' Varsity Soccer players, as well as a boy each on the JV soccer team this year. We are constantly being asked questions by the new Varsity players' parents about what to expect. They ask us these questions because we have "been there, done that, and gotten the t-shirt." We have experienced Varsity soccer first-hand so our opinions and advice are respected because they come from experience.

Anytime we need advice, we want information from someone who knows what they are talking about. In these three small books of John, we are given advice and encouragement for living in a Christ-like manner from someone who was an eyewitness to the way Christ actually lived His life. Knowing this gives these books and their author a vast amount of credibility. John was a believer and an encourager of Christ-like living, having been encouraged by Christ, in the flesh. What a treasure we have in these short little letters from the eyewitness perspective of John, the beloved.

We have tried to leave room for you to draw your own conclusions about these books of John. Most of the success of this study depends on you, our willing participants. When you open your books each week, start your time of study with prayer. Ask God to reveal His truth for you that day. As you study, allow yourself to be challenged, and be open to new growth as you dig deep in His Word. Remember, our purpose in writing this is not just for the sake of more "knowledge." There is nothing wrong with knowledge, but the key is allowing the knowledge to change you. The purpose is getting to KNOW God's Word so that you can APPLY God's Word.

We would like to give you a few hints for enhancing your study time. As you read John's letters, and learn from them, there may be times you would like to take further notes or write down more of your thoughts. So, we have included a page for notes at the end of each lesson. A dictionary might come in handy as well. If you are new to Bible study there may be some words you would like to look up in order to better understand what you are reading. In the same token, some of us have done a thousand and one Bible studies, and we like to skim over words and act like we have an understanding. I encourage you to not rush through and miss out on a blessing. If you are a little unsure of a definition, no one will know if you look it up, unless you tell! Be brave...strive to be a curious student! No one knows it all. Really! In addition to a dictionary, having a copy of the Bible in different versions will give you further insight as you study. We reference *THE MESSAGE* version of the Bible several times, so this particular one would be especially helpful to you. If you don't already own one, getting this version would be a great purchase; however, it is also easily accessible on the Internet.

In every lesson you find Deeper Still questions and activities. These are designed to give you an opportunity to study further. Do not feel pressured to do them. Just look at them as bonus material—if you have time at the end of your study each week, you can always go back and do them. To help with the Deeper Still questions, and any other questions you need further study on, we have included a resource page in the back of the book. We have taken the time to list a few resources that could be helpful in your study time.

Being able to remember Scripture is very beneficial. In those moments when you are in a difficult situation or challenge and you are without your Bible, the Word of God that you have hidden in your heart can be a great comfort. It can also help when someone else comes to you with a need. You never know when you might need to call upon the Bible for help. Short of carrying your Bible with you everywhere you go, having verses of it memorized is the only way to be certain you will have it with you at all times. To encourage you to keep His Word close, we have included Memory Verses at the beginning of each lesson, with a fill-in-the-blank at the end to test your memory! Note that these are the verses we would suggest you memorize, but if there is another verse that speaks to your heart or another version that would be easier for you to memorize, use it instead! This is just another way of putting this book of the Bible to work in your life!

I wish you could have joined us on the journey of writing this study. We are always amazed at how the truth of God's Word comes alive in all of our lives as we write. Our faith, our prayer lives, and our dependency on the Lord are most definitely put to the test during these times of study. 1, 2, & 3 John are books that challenge you to dig deep for that consistent walk with the Lord. John challenges us to know what we believe and to be on the lookout for anyone who tries to lead us astray. He sets the standard high for believers in Christ to look like, love like, act like, and speak like Christ. They are books that remind you who Christ was from an eyewitness perspective, and then take it further in asking us all to live by Christ's example.

I pray that as you read and study what God gave us in these books, you will begin to see Christ through the eyes of John, and in the process, begin to look more and more like Him. Be prepared to be challenged and open yourself up to some self-examination. I cannot wait to hear what happens when you walk this journey with John. You will be amazed at what happens when you begin to apply God's Truth to your life. Will those you come in contact with see Jesus in you? The only way this world will have an eyewitness experience with Christ is to see Him in His followers!

On the lookout for Jesus,

Crystal Colp

AN INTRODUCTION

1st, 2nd, and 3rd John are believed to have been written by the Apostle John when he was in his 90s, nearing the end of his life. Most scholars agree that all the books were written by John based on similarities between them and the Gospel of John. Written around A.D. 90, these books are considered to be some of the most intimate writings in the Bible as a whole, aside from the Song of Solomon.

John is often thought of as one of Jesus' closest friends. If you look closely at a picture of The Last Supper, you will notice one of the disciples leaning on Jesus. That is John, "The Beloved Disciple." He was the first cousin of Jesus, his mother being Mary's sister, Salome. He was clearly a major participant in the events of Jesus' life here on earth. He was entrusted with the care of Jesus' mother after the crucifixion, and cared for her until her death.

John was a fisherman in business with Peter, Andrew, and his brother James. His father was Zebedee, who was also a fisherman in Galilee. John, along with Peter, Andrew, and James, left the family business behind to become a disciple of Christ. After the death, burial, and resurrection of Jesus, John pastored a church in Ephesus. Later, by rule of the Roman Emperor, John was exiled to the island of Patmos. The Emperor, Domitian, saw John as a threat to his throne and had him exiled. The book of Revelation is thought to have been written by John during his time in exile. After his release, John returned to Ephesus. He birthed churches throughout Asia, until old age kept him from continuing. He died peacefully in Ephesus, the last of the original 12 disciples of Jesus to die.

The Gospel of John, 1, 2, and 3 John, and the book of Revelation are said to have been penned by John the Apostle. Throughout his writings we see his consistent longing for God's people to love one another. He repeated the phrase, "Little children, love one another!" constantly as he neared the end of his life. This substantiates the belief that John thought this was the Lord's most important commandment.

John wrote these letters to his "dear children," (1 John 2:1) who are not one specific group. On the contrary, this is more of a family letter written to several churches or the body of believers at large. He felt they needed assurance of the fact that Christ was the Son of God at a time when Christians were listening to false teachers and challenging the truth of Christ. The goal was to expose these false teachers and give followers a reason to believe in salvation. Dangerous heresy was spreading like wildfire, and John wanted to put a stop to it any way he could. John loved Jesus and His church; protecting it and the message of the gospel of Jesus Christ became his main goal as evidenced in these three irreplaceable books.

Deeper Still

To get to know the Apostle John better and for further background information **read the Gospel of John.**

Before You Begin

In order to gain an overview of 1, 2, & 3 John read them from start to finish in one sitting.

Don't be intimidated by the fact that we are asking you to read three books. All three "books" are only seven chapters in length when put together. Reading these texts in several different versions of the Bible can be helpful and can give you greater insight. As you read, **write down your initial thoughts. Be sure to look for any key words that recur in the Scriptures as you read and write those down as well.**

Notes:

LESSON 1

Read 1John 1:1-4.

Write down your initial thoughts.

_____

_____

_____

Write down any key words you see throughout the text.

_____

_____

Don't you just love the tone of John's letter? His passion is almost palatable. You get a sense that he is very concerned that the reader understands that he is trustworthy. From the very beginning that immediately puts the reader at ease. What he is saying is truth. Not just because he said so, but because he, along with many others, had seen Jesus, heard Him, and even touched Him. John was truly dwelling in reality as he wrote this letter. Right at the start John gives two reasons why he has a desire to pass on this good news.

Read verse 3. According to this verse, what was John's first reason for sharing?

_____

_____

What do you think this means?

_____

_____

In verse 3, his first reason is "so that you also may have fellowship with us. And our fellowship is with the Father and with His Son, Jesus Christ" (NIV). The basis of his first reason for sharing this truth is relational in nature. He wants the readers to get past the superficial relationships based in second-hand knowledge only and begin new relationships with other believers and God Himself that are rooted in the truth—the truth of John's eyewitness account of the Son of God. Knowing the truth and living IN the truth leads to changed relationships. Now let's look at reason number two.

Read verse 4. According to this verse, what was John's second reason for sharing?

_____

_____

_____

What do you think this means?

_____

_____

_____

His second reason is all about joy...REAL joy! Have you ever noticed that REAL joy is contagious? And REAL joy comes from knowing the REAL truth! The truth of the Gospel of Jesus Christ is life transforming. Transformed lives bring about transformed relationships (i.e. fellowship), which in turn bring about joy. This joy is only completed when Jesus is the foundational truth that we are rooted and grounded in.

It seems that from the beginning the church was challenged by people outside and inside the church who denied the incarnation of Jesus and were not rooted in the foundational truth of Christ. The word incarnation simply means God becoming man. It is this belief in the incarnation, along with the belief in the resurrection of Jesus that sets Christians apart from every other religion and understanding of life. John knew this was a fundamental truth that must be grasped and accepted with NO reservations.

Deeper Still

Using other Bible study tools, look up references in the Scriptures about incarnation in both the Old and New Testament. Make notes on what impresses you about the OT prophecies and about ways they were fulfilled in the accounts of Jesus' life.

_____

_____

_____

John had no doubt that Jesus was both God and man. Read John 1:14. In your own words, what does it say?

_____

_____

_____

The disciples had actually seen Jesus in the flesh. They had witnessed His glory up close and personal. Because of this the disciples were charged by Jesus to share their firsthand knowledge of Him with the world (John 15:27). He wanted this story shared so all might know that the incarnation of Jesus is a historical fact, not a myth or a fabrication by men—a truth established by eyewitnesses. Just as we accept any other event in history as truth, we must accept that the incarnation of Jesus, or God becoming man through Jesus, is undeniably true. This is the truth we must be witnesses for!

Look up the following verses and write down what you learn about being witnesses of Jesus:

2 Peter 1:16-18–

_____

_____

Luke 1:1-2–

_____

_____

Acts1:1-3–

_____

_____

John 10:25–

_____

_____

John 15:24–

_____

_____

Do you think you would live your life differently if you had actually seen Jesus, touched Him, spoken with Him, and walked with Him the way John did?

_____

_____

_____

We could probably say we would be different if we had lived then and witnessed the ministry of Jesus in person. I think we all have had doubts, and struggle to live our lives in relationship to Him. I know I have often thought my faith experience and my relationship with Jesus would be much different if I could just have seen Him in person.

The disciples did have that firsthand experience and their testimony was based in those experiences. We, however, sell ourselves short when we fail to recognize the firsthand knowledge we have of the moments Jesus has shown up in our lives and left evidence of His hand at work. We too have a testimony of how we have heard Him speaking to us, seen Him at work in our lives, and been touched by Him, even though we often fail to recognize it.

Where's the point? When something exciting happens in our life, we can't wait to share it with those we love. As a matter of fact, we can get so excited that we are not afraid to share it with perfect strangers. Why then do we fail to apply that same level of excitement when it comes to sharing what God is up to in our lives? You see, just as John had an eyewitness account to testify to, SO DO WE!

Write down how you have seen Jesus, heard His voice, and been touched by Him. This is your testimony...your eyewitness account!

_____

_____

_____

Your eyewitness account, or your testimony, gives encouragement to others, just as John's words were meant to give courage to the readers of his letter. This encouragement brings about a level of intimacy among believers that can only result in a new level of fellowship. I believe one of John's goals was to bring about a camaraderie that would in turn produce a strong bond amongst believers. This bond could enable them to weather the storms the church of that day was experiencing. The fact is that the church was under attack from false teachers and heresy was running rampant.

> "What intensified this problem was that these false teachers had once been an active part of the fellowship which John's readers were continuing to enjoy. But because their "new" teaching was so contrary to the truths of the gospel, they had to part company with the faithful. As you can well imagine, those who remained in the true fellowship were unsettled and shaken by the defection of these new teachers and needed to be reassured. But in the process, the others also needed to be exposed for what they truly were—unbelieving heretics."[1]

This problem was widespread and John's letter contains advice that would not only protect the church but also the individual believer. One piece of advice was: Fellowship is important. Fellowship with Jesus and fellowship with other believers brings strength to our lives. In other words, there is strength in numbers!

Read the following verses. Write down in your own words what they have to say about fellowship with Jesus and with other believers.

Matthew 18:20–

_____

_____

John 15:1-5–

_____

_____

Ephesians 4:3-6–

_____

_____

Hebrews 10:24-25–

_____

_____

There is so much negativity around us every day. The church of today is still under attack. Followers of Jesus Christ in the United States are still persecuted in the work place, at school, in our own homes, and even martyrdom (Christians being killed because of their faith) is still a very real threat to believers in other countries.

Write down any false teachings you have come across as you have walked through your faith journey.

_____

_____

_____

Do you think there are heretics (people who teach untruths about Jesus) today? If so, give an example.

_____

_____

_____

As we walk through life we will undoubtedly encounter moments when Jesus, or faith in Him will be discussed in a manner that is false. We will be faced with moments when the banner of Truth must be raised high.

Has your faith ever been tested? If so, give an example.

_____

_____

_____

Deeper Still

Our country is slowly fading away from God's leadership. Do more research on false religions and the effect they are having on the Christian community and the world at-large. Write down what you find.

_____

_____

_____

_____

If your faith has never been challenged, hang on because it will happen at some point. We must know what we believe and why we believe it. The only way to face these struggles with unbending resolution is to face them with our arms wound tightly around the person of Jesus Christ, His Word, and other believers. Living in a lost and dying world is difficult. We must strive to reach the lost of our world, but at the same time we must also reach for growth and strength within a body of believers. John was right to encourage fellowship within the church.

What does the word fellowship mean to you?

_____

_____

_____

_____

Read 1 Corinthians 1:9. What do you learn about "fellowship" from this verse?

_____

_____

_____

_____

Is fellowship important to believers? Why or why not?

_____

_____

_____

_____

Fellowship looks different to everyone, and is usually affected by a person's personality type and family environment. Maybe for you it means coffee, doughnuts, and potluck dinners in a large group. Or maybe your version of fellowship is a one-on-one friendship. The word "fellowship" in the Greek actually comes from the word _koinonia_, which means the spiritual union of the believer with Christ. Looking at it that way, we can assume the common union believers have with Christ should bring about a deep connection with one another. Attending church on a regular basis is one place to find that union with other believers as well as a place to strengthen your union with Christ.

Deeper Still

Look up the following verses and write down what we gain by being a part of a church and by having fellowship with one another:

Acts 2:42-47–

_____

_____

Hebrews 10:24-25–

_____

_____

1 John 4:12–

_____

_____

Hebrews 3:13–

_____

_____

Galatians 5:13-14–

_____

_____

Romans 15:14–

_____

_____

Romans 12:10–

_____

_____

Ephesians 4:32–

_____

_____

1 Corinthians 12:21-26–

_____

_____

In his bestseller, *The Purpose Driven Life,* Rick Warren lists fellowship as one of the five reasons God created us. *"All of us are more consistent in our faith when others walk with us and encourage us. The Bible commands mutual accountability, mutual encouragement, mutual serving, and mutual honoring."*[2]

If you are avoiding church because of a previous bad experience, says Jill Briscoe, it is like *"refusing to seek medical care because you once went to a doctor who was a quack.* [3]

Do you think you can enjoy spiritual fellowship with God and yet not with other believers? Why or why not?

The reality is that some people avoid church like the plague because of a bad experience. So while we are on the subject of fellowship, we must not overlook the fact that we are all imperfect. Because none of us are perfect, we will not have perfect relationships; even church-going believers will disappoint us at times. This is why it is absolutely necessary to remember that Jesus Christ is the one who should be on the pedestal and not any earthly relationship. Heartache is sometimes a natural byproduct of being in relationship with others, but joy comes from the good we find in those people who are genuine, ready, willing, and able to walk through life with us in union with Christ. Friendship and fellowship bring joy when they are based in a growing, thriving, vibrant walk with the Lord.

Do you have friendships and fellowship times with other believers that bring you joy? If so, write down an example of how those relationships have brought you joy. If not, what do you think is holding you back?

_____

_____

The early church, during the days of John, enjoyed fellowship with one another. Again, John encouraged this because he firmly believed that it would bring them joy and that they would be stronger as a result.

What do the following verses have to say about how the early church practiced Christian fellowship?

Acts 2:44-47

_____

_____

Hebrews 10:23-25

_____

_____

Participating in a group Bible study is one way to fellowship with other believers, and it is also a source of fellowship with Jesus Himself! You WILL find joy in this fellowship if you are willing to look!

> Jesus said, "Until now you have not asked for anything in my name. Ask and you will receive, and your joy will be complete" John 16:24 (NIV).

In Summary

Now, take some time to go through the text one more time (1John 1:1-4). After studying it a little deeper, write down what you learned from each portion of Scripture. How can you apply what you have learned to your own life?

1:1–_____

_____

1:2– _____

_____

1:3–_____

_____

1:4– _____

_____

Application

In the book of 1 John, as a whole, *John shared with the readers three tests of faith: a moral test—meaning if we obey His commands we belong to God; a social test—meaning if we love one another we belong to God; and a theological test—meaning if we truly believe that Jesus is the Son of God, the Savior of the world and that he became flesh and dwelt among us, we belong to God (Taylor, et al., Becoming, 1374).* This week, as you end your study time, ask yourself if you belong to God based on these three tests. If you cannot answer with certainty that you do in fact belong to Him, then spend some time in prayer, making sure.

If you have never accepted Him as your Savior, now is the best time to take that step. Turn to page 122 and follow the steps you find there to become a follower of Jesus Christ so that you can say, I BELONG TO HIM! After you have made this all-important decision, go on to the following paragraph in the Application portion of this week's study.

If you can say with certainty that you belong to Him, write a prayer asking that He continue to give you strength for the journey of life. Then as the week progresses, look for ways to fellowship with other believers, and write down the joy that is brought to your life through those moments.

Memory Verse

"We proclaim to you what we have _____ and _____,

so that you also may have _____ with us. And our

_____ is with the Father and with His Son, Jesus

Christ. We write this to make our_____ complete."

1 John 1:3-4 (NIV)

LESSON 2

Read 1 John 1:5-2:14

Write down your initial thoughts.

_____

_____

_____

Write down any key words you see throughout the text.

_____

_____

_____

In 1 John 1:5-7 and 1 John 2:9-11 John uses the words light and darkness to describe our spiritual condition.

_____

_____

_____

As I was reading this passage all I could think about was a Sunday school song I learned many (many!!) years ago. "This little light of mine. I'm gonna let it shine. This little light of mine, I'm gonna let it shine. Let it shine. Let it shine. Let it shine." What a simple message and a simple command. As 1 John says if we believe in the message of Jesus Christ then we cannot "hide it under a bushel—NO!!" **—Jacki**

An _NIV_ study note said that walking in the light versus walking in the darkness is really a lifestyle choice. I had never thought of it that way before. Obviously it's true—our lives are filled with choices—God has given us a free will.

Look up the words "light" and "darkness" in the dictionary. Write down some of the definitions you find.

_____

_____

_____

How do the definitions you found relate to what John is saying in scripture?

_____

_____

_____

Look up the following verses on "light" and "darkness" and write down the main point of each verse:

John 8:12–

_____

_____

_____

John 12:35–

_____

_____

_____

John 3:19-21–

_____

_____

_____

Philippians 4:8-9–What should we be thinking about if we are walking in the light?

_____

_____

What does this passage promise us if we walk in the light?

_____

_____

What are some ways we can choose to walk in darkness?

_____

_____

Why do you think it is so difficult to walk in the light and obey God's commands?

_____

_____

Would you say that you are walking in the light or in the darkness?

_____

_____

Would those who know and love you the most say you are walking in the light or in the darkness?

_____

_____

Walking in the light should make a visible difference in your life. Walking the walk is more difficult than just talking the talk. The walk and the talk must go hand in hand.

1 John 1:6 is one of several verses where John indicates that saying one thing and doing another is a lie. He also uses phrases such as "the truth is not in us" to refer to wrong thoughts or actions. I get a sense that John is not a fan of hypocrites in any way, nor does he have any patience for those who refuse to learn the truth or live out the truth once they learn it. —**Erin**

Look up the following verses and write down what the Scriptures say about false professions of belief:

Titus 1:16–

_____

_____

_____

1 John 3:18–

_____

_____

_____

Are there areas in your Christian walk where you are hesitant to seek what God's Word says, because He will expect you to live it out?

_____

_____

_____

Continue reading Ephesians 4:25-32. What are some dos and don'ts when walking in the light?

_____

_____

_____

According to Ephesians 4:22-24, what should be evident when we choose to walk in the light?

_____

_____

_____

Has your life ever been affected by a person saying one thing and doing another? If you feel comfortable doing so, write down your experience and how it affected you (Please omit specific names or other specifics that might give too much information as to who this person was, in order to protect them and you).

_____

_____

_____

_____

Seeking the Lord and applying His Word to our lives can be difficult. He never said walking in the light would be easy; however, He does promise results!

Read 1 John 1:7 and write down the two results or by-products of walking in the light.

_____

_____

_____

After John gives us the good news about walking in the light and what we gain from it, he then reverts back to his previous thoughts on hypocrisy and sin in verses 8-10. He seems very intent on addressing these issues. He makes it perfectly clear that we all have sinned. But more importantly he wants us to understand that sin need not rule our lives. We have the power to overcome through the blood of Jesus. When we confess our sin, He is faithful to forgive our sin and clean us up…the choice is yours to make.

It must have been important to John to address the area of sin because the heretics of the day were claiming that their immoral actions were not sinful. Somehow they had convinced themselves that they were sinless. However, it was not then, nor is it now possible, to live a life free of sin. We do not have the power within us to never sin. Only Jesus was perfect—only Jesus lived a perfect life. But despite sin, we have hope.

> We don't like to recognize our ruin, but that's where Jesus begins. Once we're honest with ourselves about who we are, then God can begin to remold our hearts…total surrender.[4]

—Max Lucado

What do the following verses say about our sin?

Luke 17:1-4–

_____

_____

John 1:29–

_____

_____

Romans 3:23–

_____

_____

Romans 6:23–

_____

_____

Romans 5:8–

_____

_____

If you look further into our original text in 1 John by looking at Chapter 2 verses 9-11, you will see that John points out one sin in particular. He has a deep concern for believers to live a pure life, forgiven of sin, walking the walk, and talking the talk. This pure life must include the way we relate to other people.

What is the sinful behavior that John points out in 1 John 2:9-11? What does he say will happen if we walk in the darkness of this sin?

This sinful behavior is no different than any other sinful behavior. Sin is sin, and because of the sin in our lives we need a Savior. John has good news in this letter. We do have a Savior, and His name is Jesus Christ!

Read 1 John 2:1-6 again. Who is our advocate?

_____

_____

_____

What is the role of an advocate?

_____

_____

_____

Deeper Still

What does the phrase "atoning sacrifice for our sins" mean?

_____

_____

Did you realize that God the Father directed all His wrath against our sin away from us and toward Jesus, His one and only Son? This should be an overwhelming thought. Jesus stood in the gap for us. Even more than that, He died for us.

Read John 3:16-17. Do you have any new insight regarding this beloved Scripture?

_____

_____

_____

Read the rest of the 3rd chapter of John.

_____

_____

_____

I find it ironic that in order to walk in the light, we must first admit we were in the dark. In order to live a pure life, we must admit to the sinful life. This is part of the process of surrender. Jesus can save us, but we first must admit we are lost and in need of saving. Humility plays a big role!

The revelation here is that NOBODY is perfect. If we were perfect there would have been no need for the sacrifice. God wants to know that we are aware of our sin. This means we are also aware of our need for Jesus—aware that we have a constant need for His guidance in our lives. Pure living is a journey; it is only through constant participation with God that we can continue on this journey.

Salvation is a free gift that we work **out** (_Notice that I did NOT say we work **for** our salvation._) with God as His light reveals the junk in our lives that the darkness had hidden from view. Salvation is not an overnight transformation but rather a constant growth process, as we trust Almighty God enough to let Him into the dark corners of our lives to clean them out one by one! We must trust that He knows what He is doing and give Him an all-access pass to every room in our heart.

Taking the initial step of confessing Him as your Lord and Savior is the beginning of this journey on the road toward being more and more Christ-like! Trust Him enough to know that He can help you when you mess up. Trust His heart enough to know He still loves you and that His love is WAY BIGGER than the sin you just committed. Ask Him to forgive your failings, dust yourself off, and get on with it! Just make sure you are learning from your mistakes and growing up in Him. If you are truly growing, you will find over time that you are "messing up" or sinning less and less. Don't give up.

Put yourself in a place to be encouraged, lifted up, and challenged so that growth becomes the expectation instead of the exception. This is a statement that every believer should buy into. It doesn't matter where you are on the relationship journey with Christ. You should be growing and putting yourself in positions to experience growth whether you are new in the faith, a "teenager" in the faith, or an "old-timer" in faith years!

Read Hebrews 5:13-14. Write down what you learn from reading this portion of Scripture.

_____

_____

_____

If you feel like you have arrived in your faith journey and you don't have any growing left to do…well friend, you probably need to hear this more than anyone else. Stagnation is one of the worst enemies of faith. Just as our physical body needs activity and our physical minds need stimulation, so our spiritual walk needs constant stretching. Strive to look more and more like Christ every day, until He comes to take you to be with Him for eternity.

John ends this portion of our text along these same lines. He is encouraging all generations in their faith. In 1 John 2:12-14 he repeats himself twice.

In your own words what is John saying to children, fathers, and young men in verses 12-14 of our text?

_____

_____

_____

Why do you think John repeated himself?

_____

_____

_____

Sometimes we repeat ourselves because we wonder if the individual we are talking to is really listening. John is no different. He is speaking truth and he wants to make sure the readers understand that what he is saying is very important. He is reminding the reader and us of valuable truth. This truth is the identity of who we are in Christ. The world may be sending us other messages about who we are, but he meets us right where we are and gives us a new identity. God's love and acceptance is all inclusive, regardless of age, when we accept Him as our Savior. God writes to all ages because we come to Him as individuals. Each man/woman in this passage is responsible for his/her own faith and obedience. We are not forgiven because our parents are forgiven, nor are our children forgiven when we are.

This is a personal decision that every individual must own. When you own it, take hold of it with both hands and don't let go. The real truth is…you are a child of The King! Find strength for your walk in that truth!

In Summary

Now, take some time to go through the text one more time (1John.1:5—2:14). After studying It a little deeper, write down what you learned from each portion of Scripture to your own life?

1:5-7– _____

_____

1:8-10– _____

_____

2:1-6– _____

_____

2:7-11– _____

_____

2:12-14– _____

_____

Application

What do you believe your identity is in Christ? Have you allowed the world to tell you that your identity is something different? We have probably all had an identity crisis at some point in our lives. This week your Application exercise is all about finding a renewed sense of identity in Christ.

Write down the words **"I am a child of The King, and today I commit to walk in the light of who He is in me!"** on a card or piece of paper and put it someplace where you will see it several times during each day of this week. Seeing this statement at the beginning of your day would be especially beneficial.

Make sure to spend time in prayer asking the Lord to give you strength to live in that truth every day. At the end of the week write how this exercise made you feel or how you feel it benefitted you.

Memory Verse

"My dear children, I write to you so that you will not _____ But if

anybody does _____, we have one who speaks to the Father in

our _____—Jesus Christ, the Righteous One.

He is the atoning _____for our sins, and not only for ours but

also for the sins of the whole_____."

1 John 2:1–2 (NIV)

Notes:

_____

_____

_____

_____

_____

_____

_____

_____

_____

_____

_____

_____

_____

_____

_____

_____

_____

_____

_____

_____

_____

_____

_____

LESSON 3

Read 1 John 2:15-27

Write down your initial thoughts.

_____

_____

_____

Write down any key words you see throughout the text.

_____

_____

_____

In this portion of Scripture John begins by speaking to the readers about what they should love. John says we are not to love the world's ways. He is specific about lust, envy, and pride. He is reinforcing his primary message that our love for God must be real and should rise above the world and all of its temptations. If we truly love God, then our actions will prove it. As believers we struggle every day between what the world expects of us and our love for God.

Why do you think we struggle to choose God's way versus the world's way?

_____

_____

_____

Why do you think the things of this world are so tempting?

_____

_____

_____

Was there a time in your life when you were caught up in worldly things? If so, explain.

_____

_____

_____

What steps do you think we need to take to become more heavenly minded and less distracted by worldly things?

_____

_____

_____

When others observe your life choices would they say you are heavenly minded or worldly minded?

_____

_____

_____

I am reminded as I read these verses that someone is always watching us. We may not see them or know they are watching, but they are. We have an incredible ability to influence others for the kingdom when we choose to focus on heavenly rewards and not on worldly rewards. Just today my devotion was entitled "A Heavenly Perspective." (Now how timely was that? A coincidence you say? I don't think so!!) The writer went on to say that even simple choices such as how we spend our time or our money or our energy can become opportunities with great promise. Everything we do today matters forever. It all counts toward eternity; however, even when we make heavenly choices, we may suffer earthly rejection. But Jesus offers great encouragement in Luke 6:22-23 when He says, "Count yourself blessed every time someone cuts you down or throws you out, every time someone smears or blackens your name to discredit me. What it means is that the truth is too close for comfort and that person is uncomfortable. You can be glad when that happens—skip like a lamb, if you like!—for even though they don't like *it, I do...and all heaven applauds. And know that you are in good company; my preachers and witnesses have always been treated like this."* (The Message)—**Jacki**

Think about the idea that heaven is applauding when you choose to be heavenly minded. Don't you just love the thought of that? If you do, then "skip like a lamb!"

Have you ever experienced rejection for making heavenly choices? How did it make you feel?

_____

_____

_____

John's heart is heavy for the readers of his letter. He knows these choices are not easy, but he also knows there is urgency to his message. He begins verse 18 by calling them "Dear Children." He wants us, the readers, to know how much he cares and how he sees us. It is quite possible he did this to get the reader's attention and to earn the reader's trust, so the reader would understand and accept the urgency of the message.

Read 1 John 2:18-19 and then rephrase the verses in your own words.

_____

_____

_____

What is the last hour?

_____

_____

What is the sign of the last hour that John is pointing out?

_____

_____

There is much discussion surrounding the idea of "The Antichrist." *(We will not get into discussions surrounding the idea of The Antichrist during this Bible study. If you have questions regarding the theology of The Antichrist, we suggest that you do your own personal research and talk with someone that you consider a student of God's Word.)* John is directly talking about antichrists in this portion of Scripture. Even though the same word is used, there is a difference here, though it is subtle. You see the difference is in the capitalization of the word antichrist. One is capitalized and one is not. John is focused on the word antichrist that is NOT capitalized. This concept of an antichrist refers to the intention of a person and not the person himself. Any of us can live in such a way that we exemplify the word antichrist. For example, I could say, "That child is the devil." I do not mean that the child is the actual Devil. I mean that the child is acting like a devil or has bad behavior. The principle is the same here.

What do you think it looks like for someone to act like an antichrist?

_____

_____

_____

An antichrist is defined to be a false Christ, an enemy of Christ, a deceiver, or one pretending to be Christ.

_____

_____

_____

What are these people doing that makes John say they are antichrists?

_____

_____

_____

Can you think of a current example of a pretender or a deceiver claiming to be a follower of Christ? If so, explain.

_____

_____

_____

Can you think of a time when your actions may have led someone to consider you a pretender? Explain.

_____

_____

_____

Read the following scriptures and write down how they remind you of the instructions given in 1 John 2:15-19:

Romans 16:17-18–

_____

_____

_____

2 Corinthians 11:13–

_____

_____

_____

John gave instructions to be on the lookout for people who would lead us astray, or antichrists. He continues on with this line of thinking in verses 20-23 of our text. Generally speaking lots of people throw the word "god" around. They may say, "I believe in God," but the true test of their faith is revealed by their relationship with Jesus Christ. John reminds them: "But, you know the truth." The readers have no excuse to follow deceivers. In one Bible concordance there were over 100 verses where Jesus used the phrase, "I tell you the truth." He may have known there would be antichrists for all time— people who would claim to "know" the truth but deny that Jesus really was who He said He was. This is an important reminder that we need to know what we believe and why we believe it. And we must be on the lookout for those who could lead us astray.

John wanted the readers of his letter to watch out for antichrists, identify them, and to be reminded of what they believed. He also wanted them to gain a new sense of assurance in their own salvation. 1 John 2:24-28 address-es that exact subject matter. John is assuring the readers that if you have a relationship with Jesus Christ and believe Him to be the Son of God, the one and only God, then you can be assured of heaven. He then goes on to affirm their salvation by writing about their anointing through the Holy Spirit, and encouraging them in verse 28 to "continue in Him" (NIV1984).

Deeper Still

What does the word "anointed" mean?

_____

_____

What does "continue in Him" mean?

_____

_____

The word "abide" means the same thing as "continue in Him." The defini-tion of abide is to continue in a state or place; to endure.

Read the following verses and write down what they have to say about abiding in Christ:

John 15:4-10–

_____

_____

_____

2 John 1:9–

_____

_____

_____

1 John 2:24–

_____

_____

_____

John seems particularly interested in this concept of abiding in Christ. All the scriptures referenced above were written by John!

> In my life, abiding in Christ looks different at different times. The similarity is always an attachment or proximity to Christ. Sometimes I am clinging tightly and need His comfort. Sometimes we are walking arm-in-arm with everyday conversation, intimate but casual. And sometimes I am moving about, thinking more about the day than Him, but His presence is in the room with me and His Spirit guides my thoughts and movements, especially when I am tempted to be lazy and selfish. Abiding is never a short-term word. It reflects a steadfast partnership and a willingness to join in partnership with Christ, trusting His boundaries and His promises. **—Erin**

What are some practical ways to abide or "continue in" Christ?

_____

_____

_____

One practical way to continually abide in Christ is to spend time studying His Word, just like you are doing now. We can also learn a lot from and be encouraged by pastors, teachers, other believers, and The Holy Spirit.

"John is not ruling out human teachers (in 1 John 2:26-27). At the time he wrote, however, Gnostic teachers were insisting that the teaching of the apostles was to be supplemented with the 'higher knowledge' that they (the Gnostics) claimed to possess. John's response was that what the readers were taught under the Spirit's ministry through the apostles not only was adequate but was the only reliable truth."[5]

The apostles were operating under the power of the Holy Spirit. Through salvation we receive the power of the Holy Spirit in our own lives. In the New Century translation the anointing or receiving of the Holy Spirit is called "a gift." It goes on to say, "His gift teaches you about everything, and it is true not false."

Can you think of a really great gift you have gotten in your lifetime? Explain.

_____

_____

_____

You probably took extra special care of that gift…guarded it, kept it in a safe place, and cherished it from time to time. This is exactly how we should handle the gift of The Holy Spirit. We should keep Him near, listen to Him, heed Him, and trust Him to make a difference in our lives.

The Holy Spirit may be a dimension of the Trinity that you don't recognize or claim. In my mind it is the still small voice sitting on my shoulder, whispering in my ear. Can you think of a time when a friend came to mind and you decided to pick up the phone and call him or her, only to discover that he or she was in the midst of a very difficult struggle and needed your encouragement? That friends, is the work of the Holy Spirit. That is God nudging you to reach out and make a difference in someone's life. Personally, I have long given the Holy Spirit credit for prompting me to make an appointment with my eye doctor in 1998. I had no particular issues with my eye; I just kept being reminded that I needed to go in for a routine exam. That's when a malignant tumor was found in my eye. It was a very serious issue, but treatment options were available. They probably would not have been effective if the tumor had been bigger. And just recently The Holy Spirit prompted me to get a full body scan for moles. I didn't necessarily think I had any of particular concern but was continually prompted to make an appointment. The doctor found 2 suspicious moles that ended up being precancerous, and they were found in time to remove them safely. I say all this to *strongly encourage you to listen, really listen, to the voice of God. If He is telling you to flee…then FLEE. If He puts someone on your heart to pray for…then PRAY. If someone comes to mind for no earthly reason, be heavenly minded and CALL THEM!* **—Jacki**

Write down a time when you felt the Holy Spirit prompted you to action.

_____

_____

_____

The Holy Spirit not only prompts us toward action, but He also alerts us to false teachers and causes us to put on "the brakes." The Holy Spirit guides us into knowing and claiming the truth about Jesus. It is that Holy Spirit that we should rely on as we navigate our way through this world, so that we do not fall prey to false teachers. John ends this portion of Scripture saying just that, you don't need someone to hold your hand; you just need to find confidence in the truth that you already know! Be a picture of Jesus Christ, who lives in you, to the world. Allow Him to be your guide!

What changes would you have to make in your life in order to be a picture of Jesus?

_____

_____

_____

_____

Write down what a typical day would look like if you were being guided by the Holy Spirit?

_____

_____

_____

How would your life look different from the way you are living right now?

_____

_____

_____

End your study time today by reading 1 John 2:28 and putting it in your own words.

_____

_____

_____

_____

_____

In Summary

Now, take some time to go through the text one more time (1 John 2:15-28). After studying a little deeper, write down what you learned from each portion of Scripture.

How can you apply what you have learned to your own life?

2:15-17– _____

_____

2:18-19– _____

_____

2:22-25– _____

_____

2:26-27– _____

_____

2:28– _____

_____

Application

Pray and ask the Holy Spirit to guide your life in a real way this week. As you feel His guiding hand during the week, write down what was going on and how His presence made a difference.

_____

_____

_____

_____

Memory Verse

"Don't love the world's_____. Don't love the world's _____.

Love of the world squeezes out love for the_____. (16) Practical-

ly everything that goes on in the world—wanting your own_____,

wanting everything for _____, wanting to appear _____—

has nothing to do with the_____. It just _____ you from

Him. (17) The world and all its wanting, wanting, wanting is on the way

out—but whoever does what God wants is set for_____."

1 John 2:15-17 (MSG)

Notes:

LESSON 4

Read 1 John 2:28—3:10.

Write your initial thoughts below.

_____

_____

_____

Write any key words you see throughout the text.

_____

_____

_____

John begins this portion of Scripture by issuing a challenge to us, as children of God. In verse 28, he states that we should "*Continue in him (God), so that when he appears we may be confident and unashamed before him at his coming*" (NIV).

What does the challenge "continue in him" mean to you?

_____

_____

_____

If you look at this particular verse in other translations the word "*continue*" is also translated as *abide*. In the Greek this word is a verb meaning to stay or remain, to be true to, to persevere, and to remain beside or near. *The Message* translates this statement as "*Live deeply in Christ.*" John uses this same word 43 times throughout the Gospel of John, 1 John, and 2 John. His goal seems to be to call the children of God to remain faithful. He is issuing a challenge to live a life that is truly pleasing to God, the Father. One website put it this way:

"We are to stay in Christ, not yielding to the world around us. In being firm and immovable in our walk with God, we will experience the love of God lived out through our lives. Our hearts become His dwelling place and His ours." [6]

As John goes on in verse 29 (NIV) to explain or describe those who have born of God, he makes a sweeping statement: *"...everyone who does what is right has been born of him."*

What conclusion could you jump to if you looked at this verse all by itself?

As I read 1 John 2:29, I found myself wanting to say to John, "that's a little too vague." I know a lot of people who pride themselves on living a good life, but who have never accepted Christ as their personal Savior. If this statement could identify only followers of Christ, then there would be people who have never accepted Christ as their Savior looking an awful lot like children of God. However, as I thought a bit longer I realized that if people are doing what is right, one HUGE "right thing" would be inviting Jesus into their hearts and living as children of God. So, I guess John's statement is correct in the true sense of it. I think it is very important to recognize the fact that just as walking into a McDonald's does not make me a Big Mac, doing good things does not make me a Christian. It is not what we do, it is who we belong to. If I were John's editor, I might have asked for clarification on this particular statement. This is why it is crucial that we, as followers of Jesus, become students of The Bible. I think you can see from this one verse (29) how someone could use Scripture out of context. Because I have been a student of the Word of God, I know that John did not mean that as long as I do good things I am saved. I know that accepting Jesus as my Savior AND doing what is right go hand in hand to work out my salvation. This is the spirit of John's words. John is very zealous in his desire to help us understand that we must not just profess that we love Jesus with our mouth...we must also look like Jesus so that when God Almighty comes to take us home with Him, He recognizes us!!!!
—Crystal

Now, John switches gears beginning with verse 1 of Chapter 3. He is so excited for the readers of his letter to know exactly how much God loves them. He shares with them the good news that we can now be called *"children of God."*

Have you become a child of God? If so, share the story of how that happened in your life.

What is incredible to you about the way God the Father loves you? How is it different from the way any other person has loved you?

_____

_____

_____

If not, today would be a great day to do that!! If you would like to accept Jesus as your Savior, look in the back of your book on page 122, follow the instructions there, and then share the exciting news that you are now a child of God with someone or everyone close to you!

How does the knowledge that we will see Jesus face-to-face someday affect the way you live your life today?

> I thought of my own father when I read these verses and how I often kept from doing something I shouldn't by the thought, "What will my father think of me?" In school many of my friends were restrained by fear of punishment. "My dad will kill me." But it wasn't my father's anger that I dreaded. Instead, I dreaded the disappointment in my father's eyes and the deep regret of betraying his love and trust in me. As a Christian, I know God forgives and loves me as His child, but I don't want to see sorrow in his eyes for times that I neglected his love and dishonored him in my actions and conversation. Remembering that I will soon be with Jesus gives every day heavenly promise, direction, and peace as I try to please Him in what I choose and in what I do. I live before an audience of one. —**Alice**

The way followers of Jesus choose to live their lives is different from the rest of the world, because we _live before an audience of one_. John is careful to let us know he understands that the world will not always understand the way we live. And in one phrase in verse 1 he explains it all, _"The reason the world does not know us is that it did not know Him."_

How will the world get to know Jesus?

_____

_____

_____

Name some ways that knowing God as your Father and Jesus' love has changed your lifestyle and the things you pursue today.

The way that we view life and the goals we pursue will undoubtedly change as we grow closer and closer to Christ, with the ultimate goal of looking more and more like Him every day!

If God's ultimate goal for us is to look like Christ, how do the following verses describe our destiny?

Romans 8:29–

_____

_____

Philippians 3:21–

_____

_____

1 Thessalonians 2:13-14–

_____

_____

In 1 John 3:3, John goes on to speak of the hope we have in our destiny as children of God. The hope spoken of in this verse does not refer to wishful thinking or the "cross my fingers" kind of hope. It refers to the unshakeable confidence we have in spending eternity in heaven with God almighty.

> _Just this past week my almost 97-year-old aunt died and went to be with the Lord. She was my Dad's sister and the last of her family's generation to go from life to life. What a great comfort it was to think of the wonderful reunion going on in heaven. I imagined her being greeted at the pearly gates by my dad and mom and her sister and older brother. Maybe they held her hand as she was escorted to the heavenly throne. That is the picture that takes away the sting of death. That's what the hope of heaven is all about._ —**Jacki**

In describing the hope of heaven, John explains the purifying effect that knowledge has upon those who truly believe. This is not an instant effect or change, but one that is progressive, a journey that is finally perfected when we see Jesus.

How does the Apostle Paul, in the following verses, describe this process and our part in it?

2 Corinthians 5:8-10–

_____

_____

1 Peter 1:8–

_____

_____

Philippians 3:12-14–

_____

_____

Colossians 3:1-4–

_____

_____

Knowing we are on a journey and that God will continually reveal to us what things we need to work on is a revelation that should be freeing. Studying the Bible is one way God can reveal truth about sin in our lives. John goes on in 1 John 3:4-6 to talk about this sin problem we have.

*I like to translate verse 6 as: "No one who lives in him keeps on considering sin as no big deal. No one who continues to consider sin no big deal has either seen him or known him." In considering the question: "Is it possible to **be seen as** completely without sin?" I think the answer is that through Christ, our sins are covered up to God. Not invisible, because God is God—just covered up. Can't you see Christ standing over me? Blocking the view, when God is trying to peek behind Him? Jesus* *bobs and weaves, saying, "Nothing to see here. Move on Dad...nothing going on here." OK, God knows I'm not perfect, but He's pleased that Christ is covering for me. Christ's blood cleans up my sins because I have confessed them and asked for His grace. So God the Father moves on and says, "I saw nothing but Jesus," when He was looking for Erin.* **—Erin**

Often times we allow unconfessed sin to remain in our lives simply because we are too stubborn to admit we are wrong. Other times we allow outside influences in our lives to convince us that we don't have a sin problem. We joke about someone being a bad influence in our lives, but Scripture would indicate that this notion is anything but a joke.

What is the clear command in 1 John 3:7?

_____

_____

We all are too quick to point out the bad influences in other people's lives but are less likely to see and acknowledge the less than stellar influences in our own.

Do you have anyone in your life leading you astray?

_____

_____

What steps will you take this week to correct that situation?

_____

_____

In verses 7 and 8 of our text we see that John categorizes the people in this world or the influences in our lives into two categories.

_____

_____

_____

What are these two types of people?

_____

_____

What characterizes and distinguishes the children of God from the children of the devil?

_____

_____

Deeper Still

In John 8:42-47 Jesus makes it very clear that we are considered children of the devil if we do not believe in Him (John 6:28-29).

Read this passage and answer the following questions:

Vs 42. If God were our Father, who else would we also love?

_____

_____

_____

Vs 42. Who sent Jesus to earth?

_____

_____

_____

Vs 44. How long has the devil been around?

_____

_____

_____

Vs 44. Who is the father of lies?

_____

_____

_____

Vs 47. What do we hear, if we are a child of God?

_____

_____

_____

In 1 John 3:8, John emphasizes that the devil is alive and well. As we have discussed, the devil lives in this world and often uses other people to lead us astray. He would like nothing better than to see us stop living God's way and instead, live a life of sin.

Continue to read verses 9-10 in our text. How is it possible to keep from living a life of sin, habitually practicing sin, and falling away from God?

(We will never be perfect in this life here on earth…remember, we are on a journey toward being perfected in eternity.)

What steps can we take to persevere in our walk with Jesus and keep growing in His likeness?

Jude 20-21–

_____

_____

_____

Romans 12:1-2–

_____

_____

_____

2 Peter 3:18–

_____

_____

_____

Hebrews 12:1-2–

_____

_____

_____

John knew that no one but Jesus could live a perfect life free from sin. But as children of God, we should strive to not live in continuous sin. Instead, we should strive every day to look more and more like Jesus. If you are consciously choosing to sin against God or other people then you are not doing what is right. This is a deliberate choice to ignore the new life God has given you (1 Corinthians 6:18-19). On the contrary, we should work to do what is right and love others as God loves us. John is basically asking us in 1 John 2:28-3:10 to take stock of our lives and make sure we are living in the right way and for the right things. John is asking us to consider the source. You see, in this portion of Scripture, John reminds us that God is the **source** of our love, Jesus is the **source** of our redemption, and God's Word is the **source** of knowledge that keeps us from going astray. The question now remains: ARE YOU PLUGGED IN TO THE SOURCE?

In Summary

Now, take some time to go through the text once more (1 John 2:28—3:10). After studying it a little deeper, write down what you learned from each portion of Scripture.

How can you apply what you have learned to your own life?

2:28-29– _____

_____

3:1-3– _____

_____

3:4-6– _____

_____

3:7-8– _____

_____

3:9-10– _____

_____

Application

Every day our Father wants us to draw closer to Him so that we in turn reflect more of His glory. Over the course of this week, ask Him to reveal to you anything in your life that does not honor Him.

As He speaks to you write down what He shows you as you walk the journey of looking more like Jesus this week.

Memory Verse

_"How great is the love the Father has _____ on us, that we_

_should be called _____ of God! And that is what we are! The_

_reason the world does not know us is that it did not know _____."_

1 John 3:1(NIV)

LESSON 5

Read 1 John 3:11—4:6

Write down your initial thoughts.

_____

_____

_____

Write down any key words you see throughout the text.

_____

_____

_____

John is following up the previous verses that we studied in Lesson 4 by expanding on the characteristics of Christians that show they are children of God and not children of the devil and the world. He already pointed to righteous living in contrast to habitually sinning. Now John focuses on love by contrasting it with the lack of love of the children of the devil. He uses a story of envy to illustrate the lack of love that the children of the devil have for each other. His thought is that if you are busy loving someone, then you don't have time to envy what he or she has.

Envy is a strong emotion that causes our thoughts to stray significantly from where they should be. There are many things we can be envious of—relationships, possessions, authority, opportunities, abilities—but God has chosen you to be where you are, and He has commanded you to love as a response to what He has given.

What do the following verses say about envy, love, and bitterness? Proverbs 14:30–

_____

_____

_____

1 Corinthians 13:4–

_____

_____

_____

James 3:16–

_____

_____

_____

Romans12:9–

_____

_____

_____

Hebrews12:15–

_____

_____

_____

John 13:34-35–

_____

_____

_____

Love, envy, and bitterness can be very strong emotions. John chose to high-light the emotion of envy; thereby showing what kind of destruction the lack of love caused in the lives of Cain and Abel.

Read the story of Cain and Abel in Genesis 4.
Why did Cain hate his brother?

_____

_____

What happened to Abel?

_____

_____

Did anything good result from this sad story?

_____

_____

This story is a penetrating critique of human nature. Evil people do not love well, or unconditionally when they see others doing what is right in God's eyes. Righteousness makes them feel accused, so they crucify those who are doing what is right.

What can we learn from the story of Cain and Abel that we can apply to our lives every day?

_____

_____

_____

Describe a time when envy got in the way of God's will either in your life or another's. How would replacing love with envy have changed the situation?

_____

_____

_____

Deeper Still

The story of Joseph in Genesis 37—47 also demonstrates how hatred and jealousy can lead to sinful actions. Yet in this account of Joseph, we see what man intended for evil, God intended for good. Skim over the story and list some of the good that came from God's hand of protection on Joseph.

So often people envy those that do good deeds in the world, to the point that they respond with hatred and scorn instead of gratitude when others pour out their lives in love. In 1 John 3:13, John says we should not be surprised if the world hates us. When we love God, we will not be loved by a world that exalts itself.

What do the following verses say concerning how the world feels about the children of God?

John 15:19–

_____

_____

_____

Luke 6:22–

_____

_____

_____

Even though the world hates us, what does Romans 12:1-3 tell us to do? (Try to read this passage in _The Message_ translation in addition to the translation you are using).

_____

_____

_____

While we are not to conform to the world, we are to love those who live in the world. Time and time again in Scripture we are commanded to love one another. It is usually easy to love our family and our friends. In addition, the Bible says that we are to love our enemies—ouch! This is a hard concept to get our arms around.

What does Romans 12:9-10 say about love? (Read these verses in *The Message* translation as well as in the translation you are presently using.)

_____

_____

_____

In *The Message*, Romans 12:9 says we are not to fake love—it is to be heartfelt and genuine. While we are to run from evil, we are commanded to love evildoers—genuinely love them. Wow! This is hard!

Read Romans 12:16-21. List the ways we are to love our enemies.

_____

_____

_____

From the same passage, list the ways we are to love our friends.

_____

_____

_____

The Bible speaks of love often, using the word *love* over 314 times; however, the Bible does not claim that Christians have a monopoly on love. People are created in the likeness of God and all of us have the potential to love deeply and have strong affection for our family and friends. But in 1 John 3:16-18, John teaches how the love of God demonstrates a love we cannot know or experience apart from understanding the sacrifice Jesus made in laying down His life for us.

Love shows itself in sacrifice. Jesus sacrificed His life. We sacrifice our lives through our actions, which means we sacrifice our valued time and possessions to help others, not with gushing words of no practical value to us or to the recipient. We are urged to be "living sacrifices"—to sacrifice for others daily while we are living on this earth.

Before we go any further talking about love, let's stop and try to get a working definition of the word. We learned from our text that Jesus' sacrifice is love. While this is true, the word *love* is a word used by people today in so many ways we have lost a sense of the REAL meaning, the biblical definition of love.

How would you define love?

_____

_____

_____

Do you think God's love is different from man's love?

_____

_____

_____

> *The Bible uses different Greek words for varying degrees of love. The word used in the New Testament for God's unique love is Agapao. Love is known only by the action it prompts. God's agapao love is seen in the gift of His Son and from the actions that it prompts. Obviously this is not the love of complacency or affection, that is, it was not drawn out by any excellency in its objects (Romans 5:8). It was an exercise of the Divine will in deliberate choice, made without assignable cause save that which lies in the nature of God Himself (Deuteronomy 7:7-8). The love of God is unchanging and life giving, always seeking the good of its creation. The word love in the Greek indicates a selfless concern for the welfare of others that is not called forth by any quality of "lovableness" in the person loved, but is the product of a will to love in obedience to God's command. It is like Christ's love manifested on the cross.[7]*

In contrast, the love of man is turned inward, away from relationship with God, to affection only for those who are useful to him, belong to him or are attractive or pleasing to him. Human love relates all others to itself, rather than to God, the only life giver.

John likes to write on the subject of love. I think I know why John was called "the beloved disciple"—because "he beloved everybody," wanted everyone to be loved, wanted everyone to love, and wanted to talk about love often…every single day! John does change it up a little bit when he uses contrasts as a tool to describe love and hate. In verse 18, he uses another subtle lesson in contrasts. In 1 John 3:18, he challenges the difference in loving with actions and truth in contrast to loving with words or speech.

What do you think it means to love truth?

_____

_____

_____

Does verse 18 mean that ALL words are useless?

_____

_____

_____

Again John, in his zealous nature, makes a sweeping statement that we must be careful not to take out of context. Instead, we must relate this verse to the rest of Scripture. John speaks of love and says many loving things to his readers, but he knew the value of putting action to the words that are spoken. So often we fail at this. We are guilty many times of all talk and no action.

In what ways would our world be different if we all walked the talk?

_____

_____

_____

What can you personally do this week to put love in action?

_____

_____

_____

For some of us, putting feet to our love for others comes naturally. But if we are honest, some of us struggle with it. Be careful not to condemn yourself before you even have a chance to get started. What I mean is, we always want to know if we are doing "enough" —praying enough, studying God's Word enough, serving enough, and loving enough. **How do we know?**

_____

_____

_____

Lesson 5

In 1 John 3:19-24, John answers that very question. This section of our text is for those worried overachievers with an overactive guilt reflex. Sometimes when we have a tender conscience, we can easily condemn ourselves for our imperfect love and feel unworthy of being His child, putting our heart in a state of unrest. But there is no need to live in condemnation. You can be sure that God knows a genuine heart when He sees one. He knows when your heart is turned toward Him.

An easy answer to the question of how much is enough, is to simply make sure you are moving! If you haven't started praying, studying, serving, loving—start! Don't get wrapped up in the distance before you even put on your shoes. Pray and obey and the Spirit will guide you. As John says, if you do these things, then you will have a heart that is at rest.

How would you describe a "heart at rest?"

_____

_____

_____

When we are doing what pleases Him our heart is at rest, and we can live in confidence! Part of that confidence and peace comes from a healthy prayer life and open communication with God the Father. In 1 John 3:22, John says that if our hearts do not condemn us, we can have confidence before God and receive from Him anything we ask.

This is another example of being careful not to take one verse out of context. Verses 21 through 24 are intertwined. The idea behind these verses is praying for God's will for our lives. You see, if we are in Him and He is in us, then by the Spirit He gave us we will be able to recognize the gifts given through prayer. As we pray, our human hearts may desire one thing, but the heart God has given us will desire the answer that comes from the throne of God. Sometimes that answer is hard for our earthly hearts and minds to accept, but other times the answer brings about a greater understanding of the fact that God is God and we are not. Sometimes that answer will only be understood on the other side of eternity.

> In July of 2007, our 5-year-old son passed away unexpectedly. Many prayers were offered up on his behalf while he lay in ICU on life-support. When many look at this scripture they wonder how God chooses which requests He'll answer positively. I know He chooses according to His will.

> My prayer that day was, "God, you know far more than I do. So whatever brings you more glory, Elijah's healing or his death, please do it." I believe often times this scripture may be used to make God a "genie in a bottle." But I believe that as followers of Christ our prayers must be spoken according to His will.

> In John 14:13-14 it says, "Ask in my name." To ask in His name means to ask according to His character and His will. I have faith that when a believer prays with confidence (1 John 3:21-22) & according to His will (John 14:13-14), His will is done. We must check ourselves as we pray, that we pray for His will, not our own. My fleshly will was to have my son on this earth for 60 more years, but God's plan and purpose were far greater.

> Men have returned to the family of God because of Elijah's death. People have been strengthened in their faith because of Elijah's death. But most of all, my little man will never hurt again, and he is secure with the Father for all eternity. That is what brings me peace.

> This is my heart, and what I believe to be the truth. When walking in the flesh, it is not easy to live with, but when walking according to the Spirit, it is peace. **—Jeanette Dunaway**

Any discussion on prayer, answers to prayer, and how to pray could go on and on. The main idea is that we have been commanded to pray and instructed on how to pray in the Bible. The best advice is to simply pray and allow the rest to be sorted out when we have a chance to see Jesus face-to-face in eternity.

After John makes this passing comment about prayer, he goes on to share what God's command for us is: to believe in the name of Jesus and to love one another. Then he says that if we keep these commands, we live in God and God lives in us. Immediately after making this statement he begins 1 John 4 by giving a warning about believing in every spirit. I have to wonder if he is hinting at the fact that when you are testing to see if someone is really a lover of Jesus, the first two tests should be: Do they believe in the name of Jesus? And do they love others? As a matter of fact, John states just that in verse 3 of Chapter 4.

This is the biblical version of "Don't believe everything you hear," combined with advice that I am sure every single one of our mothers gave us, "Consider the source." This applies to the self-help advisors we listen to, celebrities, or average Joes—if they do not acknowledge Jesus Christ, their advice MUST be weighed carefully.

What does the Bible say about false prophets in the following verses?

Matthew 7:15–

_____

_____

_____

Matthew 24:11–

_____

_____

_____

1 Timothy 4:1–

_____

_____

_____

2 Peter 2:1–

_____

_____

_____

How can we best protect ourselves against false prophets?

_____

_____

_____

Aside from using God's Word as a guideline, what other resources could you use to identify false teachings?

_____

_____

_____

Part of your protective shield against a world filled with false prophets is standing on the promises found in the Word of God. 1 John 4:4 offers a beautiful promise meant to encourage us during times of trouble, doubt, and fear. How comforting to know that absolutely nothing surprises God or catches Him off guard. He is greater than anything Satan can throw at us.

Read Luke 21:18 and John 16:33. What power do we have in Jesus?

_____

_____

_____

This scripture from Luke and the writings of John pick us up and dust us off by assuring us of the power we have when Christ dwells in us. Back in our text John finishes the chapter by reminding us once again that the world cannot relate to us, but God's children will see His spirit in us and will walk hand in hand with us. The key is learning to recognize what is true and what is false in the world around us. As we gain confidence in our knowledge of His Word through Bible studies like this, we will become less and less concerned about what the world thinks of us and more and more aware of our need to be completely filled with the Spirit of God so that we can live a life as an overcomer!

In Summary

Now, take some time to go through the text once more (1 John 3:11—4:6). After studying it a little deeper, write down what you learned from each portion of Scripture. How can you apply what you have learned to your own life?

3:11-15 – _____

_____

3:16-18 – _____

_____

3:19-24 – _____

_____

4:1-3 – _____

_____

4:4-6 – _____

_____

Application

Even though we ended this lesson by once again talking about false prophets, the majority of this lesson was spent talking about love. This week, practice living a life of love. It may be easy to love your family and close friends, but practice loving the unlovable. Pray for an enemy or someone who has hurt you deeply. Pray that God would bless him or her. Pray that God would give you a genuine heart of love for that person. Write your prayers here. If you don't feel comfortable writing down that person's name in your Bible Study book then use a code. The only two people that need to know who you are praying for are you and God. At the end of the week, be sure to write down how this exercise affected you and/or your relationship with this person. Trust God for results…even if they aren't immediate. He is at work!

_____

_____

_____

_____

_____

_____

_____

_____

_____

_____

_____

_____

_____

_____

Memory Verses

"This is how we know what _____ is: Jesus Christ laid

down his _____ for us. And we ought to lay down our

_____ for our brothers and _____."

1 John 3:16 (NIV)

"Dear children, let us not love with _____ or

_____ but with _____ and in _____."

1 John 3:18 (NIV)

Notes:

Lesson 6

Read 1 John 4:7-21

Write down your initial thoughts.

_____

_____

_____

Write down any key words you see throughout the text.

_____

_____

_____

Here we go on the subject of love again. We have been here before with John. Is it just me, or does John seem to be talking in circles? God, love, you, love, God...my head is spinning when I read this portion of Scripture. I do think, however, that he gets to the point in verse 11: Since God loved us, and showed it mightily in the death of His Son, we ought to respond as proportionately as possible in our love to others.

I think it is just fine for us to repeatedly discuss this subject of love, because we live in a world that has a major misconception of what love really is. We have television shows like "The Bachelor," which we call "reality" television that highlights one man looking for "love" amongst a sea of visually beautiful women competing for his "love." This is NOT "reality." REAL love is not found in a mansion on a television show. Real love was defined by Jesus' death on a cross, where He died for all mankind. That is REALITY!

John wants to make sure we get it. He is repeating himself because he wants to make sure we are listening. John was taught by Jesus that sometimes repetition is necessary.

Read John 21:15-17. Describe this exchange between Simon Peter, and Jesus in your own words.

_____

_____

_____

_____

Jesus kept asking the same question over and over, and I suspect it had something to do with wanting to make sure His point was REALLY heard. This is reminiscent of conversations I often have with my teenage boys. They get irritated with me just as Peter got a little irritated with Jesus. Jesus wanted Peter and all those within earshot to hear the message: "If you love me (Jesus), you will love others."

What do you DO to respond to the love God has demonstrated for you?

_____

_____

_____

Loving others is not always an automatic response. We know we should respond in love toward others but sometimes love doesn't well up within us like we think it should.

When I gave birth to our first child she was everything any parent could hope for. She was healthy, beautiful, easy going...a dream baby. Unfortunately shortly after her birth I lapsed into a deep postpartum depression. It was an extremely scary time for me, my husband, and our family. I distinctly remember thinking, "I am totally void of feelings for this child." I sought medical treatment and members of our family and church family stayed with me 24/7. In spite of everything, I knew that I needed to tenderly care for our daughter. Gradually, over several weeks, the depression began to lift, and slowly but surely I developed a deep, long-lasting love for our daughter.

Years later on a TV show I heard another mother speak of how she felt during a similar postpartum depression. I sat and cried as she described all of the feelings I had experienced but could never articulate. It was a great comfort to know another mother had felt the same.

My point in sharing this story is that sometimes we need to go through the motions of loving before it resides in our hearts. Most of the time blessings follow obedience, not the other way around. If there is some-one in your life that you are having a hard time loving (husband, child, family member, friend), I encourage you to do acts of service as if you love that person. See if God allows your heart to soften in ways that could only come from Him. **—Jacki**

Can you think of a time when you had to do something for someone that you were having a hard time loving? If so, explain.

_____

_____

_____

How did you feel after you gave of your time to help this person?

_____

_____

_____

I think it is important for us to be transparent. So, let's be honest, as Jacki was honest about her experience. And, if we are going to be honest, lets just come clean and say that loving people is not always easy. In fact, sometimes it is very, very hard. It does not always come naturally to us. Sometimes it is a choice or an act of obedience.

My grandmother, who I called Memommie, grew up as an orphan. Her mom died soon after giving birth to her, and her father died just as she was turning two. Memommie lived with a cousin for a while; then, as the years went by she lived in others' homes, going from house to house until she met and married my granddaddy. As they began a fam-ily of their own, she made a conscious decision that her children and every generation following would grow up knowing what it was to be a part of a family—loved, and treasured. Memommie made a choice to live in direct contrast to the world she grew up in. She had many unanswered questions in her life, and she spent many lonely days, but the one thing she never did was decide not to love. She very well could have grown bitter from her life experience, but instead she grew beyond her experience to become one of the most loved and most loving women I have ever known. If you stepped foot in her home or within reach of her arms, you knew you were loved.

Before my husband and I were married, he came home from college with me and we went to Memommie and Granddaddy's house for lunch on Sunday. When we left, Memommie hugged him and told him she loved him. He was a bit taken back by that. He told me later that his thought was she didn't really know him, how could she love him? I explained to him that Memommie did not have to know him. It was enough that I loved him, for her to love him. I think this is what Jesus and John are trying to get across. We should love others because Jesus loves them. That should be enough.

Memommie loved without boundaries—it was not work for her, but a choice she made, every day, to live the life she had chosen many years before—one of love for everyone! She did this because, though she lived without an earthly family, God was that family. He was her mother, her father, her sustainer. Because He loved her and because He loved others, she would love them too. As she did the hard part of wanting to love, the "how to love" came easily. Jesus told Peter to feed His sheep. Memommie literally fed and clothed His sheep, but more often than not she just provided a sense of family and love for everyone she touched!

It required a lot of her energy, sometimes energy she did not have, and she often went to bed tired from a long day of cooking, serving, and having people in her home. Sometimes she was taken advantage of; sometimes her love was not reciprocated, but that did not deter her. Her love was not based on how much the other person loved her. Her love was based on how much God loved them. **—Crystal**

Crystal's Memommie chose to give from what she had received in relationship with Christ. In 1 John 4:7-8, we see that we cannot give what we have not first received, nor share with others what we haven't experienced.

Do you believe without a doubt that God loves you? If so, put your name in the following blanks: "I, _____, believe without a doubt that God loves _____!"

I pray that you really, truly know and have experienced the love of THE ALMIGHTY GOD!

Read 1 Corinthians 13:4-8 and write down how you have seen God's love displayed in your life in each way described in these verses. How has your understanding of what God's love is like changed through your life experiences?

_____

_____

_____

_____

_____

_____

_____

Read 1 John 4:9-12. How can a man/woman know the divine love of God and the truth of who He truly is?

_____

_____

_____

What was God's purpose in sending His beloved one and only Son, to become man and live here on earth?

_____

_____

_____

Read the following verses and write down what Jesus declared about what He had come to do:

John 10:9-10– _____

_____

John 11:25-26– _____

_____

Mark 1:15, 1:38–_____

_____

Mark 10:45– _____

_____

Luke 4:18-21– _____

_____

Jesus came to fulfill a purpose. Is anyone excluded and outside the redeeming love of the Father in the Son?

Read the following scriptures and write down what they say about who receives the love of Jesus and if they had to do anything to receive it.

John 3:16– _____

_____

2 Corinthians 5:18– _____

_____

2 Timothy 1:8-9–_____

_____

Jesus came to redeem the world, not because of anything we did to deserve it, but because He loved us. The beloved Son of God died for us. Now we can be called beloved. John used the term beloved as a term of endearment in 1 John 4:11. Then in verse 12 John goes on to challenge God's beloved children to love each other.

What happens according to 1 John 4:12 when we love other people as God does?

_____

_____

Has someone ever made God's love visible to you? If so, explain.

_____

_____

_____

What effect did this experience have on you?

_____

_____

_____

When you experience God's love you never forget it. God's love is vast. It is deep. It is far beyond the realm of our understanding at times, but even if we don't understand it, sharing God's love is still necessary. We must embrace the idea of love, allow it to permeate our lives, and then share it with everyone we come in contact with! That is the best way for the world to see Christ!

Read verses 13-16. Do you think that Christians are able to love in a way the world cannot? Explain.

_____

_____

_____

_____

_____

No matter how you answered the question above, there is no doubt that the love of God dwelling within the hearts of His children is a love the world can never understand apart from Him. The love relationship between our Heavenly Father and us, as His children, is beyond words. *The Message* translates 1 John 4:15 as: *"Everyone who confesses that Jesus is God's Son participates continuously in an intimate relationship with God."*

Do you think our relationship with God is something we will always feel? Explain.

_____

_____

_____

Read the following scriptures, and answer the following question: "When our hearts are cold and we lose our focus on Jesus, has He left us?"

_____

_____

_____

John 14:16-17–

_____

_____

_____

Matthew 28:20–

_____

_____

_____

Thinking that Jesus would leave us at any point would strike fear in the heart of any believer. He promises He will never leave us, so that fear is unfounded; however, many of us live with some sort of fear every day. The Word of

God says that fear and love are incompatible. Look at 1 John 4:16-18. John is not talking of the wise fear of reverence for God as God. But instead he is speaking of the fear of death and God's judgment when we face Him in eternity.

How does believing in God's love for you, as John taught in verses 16-18, vanquish all such fear?

_____

_____

_____

What does the Bible tell us about living a life of fear in the following verses?

_____

_____

_____

1 John 4:18–

_____

_____

_____

2 Corinthians 7:5-7–

_____

_____

_____

Psalm 34:4–

_____

_____

_____

Isaiah 54:14-15–

_____

_____

_____

Psalm 23:4–

_____

_____

_____

Fear is Satan's greatest weapon against us. When we live in fear we are paralyzed. We don't cry out to God or live a faith-based life. Satan would love for that to happen; he wants to render us useless and cause us to be a spiritual wasteland. When you are afraid, cry out to Jesus…He is the great Comforter. God comforts us, and we offer ourselves and our love to Him as our Father.

Read 1 John 4:19-21. What is the true test of whether or not we love God?

_____

_____

_____

Since God is the source of love, then our love for God is really His love in us, present by the Holy Spirit. The natural fruit and evidence that we love God is to love what and whom He loves.

John has essentially come full circle back to 1 John 3:16 and the commandment to love God and love others, as Christ loved us. He warned readers earlier (3:18) not to just talk about love, but to demonstrate love by what we do. The love of God always takes the initiative, and Christ Jesus is the expression of that. He came on a mission of love and continues that mission through all who belong to Him! His mission is alive in you today!

In Summary

Now, take some time to go through the text once more (1 John 4:7-21). After studying it a little deeper, write down what you learned from each portion of Scripture. How can you apply what you have learned to your own life?

4:7-8– _____

_____

4:9-12– _____

_____

4:13-16– _____

_____

4:17-18 – _____

_____

4:19-21 – _____

_____

Application

This week get your family or a friend involved in the application of God's Word. Choose a verse from this week's text to read to your family or friend. Talk to them about putting God's Word into action. Challenge them to help you come up with a way to visually show God's love to someone else this week. Write down what you chose to do to share the love of God in a tangible way. Be sure to record how applying this made you feel as a result.

_____

_____

_____

_____

_____

_____

Memory Verse

"This is how you can recognize the Spirit of _____: Every spirit that acknowledges that Jesus Christ has come in the flesh is from _____, (3) but every spirit that does not acknowledge Jesus is not from _____. This is the spirit of the _____, which you have heard is coming and even now is already in the world."

1 John 4:2-3 (NIV)

LESSON 7

Read 1 John 5

Write down your initial thoughts.

_____

_____

_____

Write down any key words you see throughout the text.

_____

_____

_____

John has been teaching the basics of Christian life: the truth of God, obedience to the truth, and surrender to the love of God. He warns readers how to recognize false teachings and antichrists. But John is not giving a list of dos and don'ts; that would lead us to legalism and away from fellowship with Christ. Instead he focuses on the positive—the victorious life for every Christian because of what God the Father has already done for us in Jesus Christ.

Read 1 John 5:1-2. John repeats two characteristics of the victorious Christian life. What are they?

_____

_____

_____

In 1 John 5:3, John explains that another way to determine victory over sin is obedience. He goes on to say that obedience is a natural result of a genuine love for God.

_____

_____

_____

When someone gives you a command, how can that be a burden or an irksome thing to do?

_____

_____

_____

Can religion be a burden? See Matthew 23:4. Give an example.

_____

_____

_____

Why are God's commands not a burden to a Christian?

_____

_____

_____

As we live in obedience what should our countenance be, and why is it important?

_____

_____

_____

Read 1 John 5:4. What victory do we have when we are born of God?

_____

_____

_____

The word "overcome," used in verses 4 and 5 of our text, occurs 24 times in the New Testament, and John uses it 21 times in his writings. It comes from a Greek word meaning _to conquer, to have victory, to have superiority, or conquering power_. It reflects a genuine victory that leads to overwhelming success, a victory that is demonstrated and seen by all. Jesus used this word to describe himself (John 16:33), and John earlier described all Christians as overcomers (1 John 2:4).

Can everyone claim this victory? Explain.

_____

_____

_____

To overcome the world is to gain victory over its sinful pattern of life, which is another way of describing obedience to God. Such obedience is not impossible for the believer because he has been born again and the Holy Spirit dwells within him and gives him strength. John speaks of two aspects of victory; (1) the initial victory of turning in faith from the world to God; (2) the continuing day-to-day victory of Christian living.[8]

As you go through your daily activities how can those closest to you know that you are an overcomer of the world?

_____

_____

Read the following verses and answer the question: How does believing in Jesus as the Son of God make us overcomers even while we still live in this world?

John 16:33–

_____

_____

_____

Romans 8:32-39–

_____

_____

_____

2 Corinthians 2:14–

_____

_____

_____

1 Peter 1:3-5–

_____

_____

_____

What do you think a victorious life looks like?

_____

_____

_____

Do you think you are living a victorious life? Why or why not?

_____

_____

_____

Deeper Still

Spend some devotional moments now, celebrating and thanking God for the victorious life Jesus has won for you. Read Psalm 118, called "A Song of Victory" (NRSV), which is thought to be regarding the coming of Christ and is the most quoted Psalm in the New Testament. It is thought that Jesus sang it with his disciples at the last supper before they left for Gethsemane. Jesus sang this before he faced death to fulfill the promise found within the Psalm itself. What are some of the "enemies and fears that Jesus has given you victory over?

Write them down and thank Him for each one.

_____

_____

_____

In verse 5 of our main text, John states that in order to live the victorious life of an overcomer, the stipulation is that we MUST believe in Jesus Christ as the Son of God. He then goes on in verses 6 and 7 to explain why we can believe in Jesus as the Son of God. Many scholars think that the reference to water and blood in 1 John 5:6 refers to the fact that Jesus was fully human. Other scholars think the water refers to the water that spilled from Jesus' side when it was pierced as He hung on the cross and the blood refers to His blood being spilled as Jesus was beaten and crucified. One other thought is that the water refers to the baptism of Jesus and the blood to the crucifixion. Regardless of the interpretation, John is making a very concise statement about the fact that Jesus is who He said He was. Verse 7 continues to further prove the validity of the Sonship of Jesus.

> _Several hundred years before Jesus, Isaiah said that there is one who is chosen; there is one who is promised. He said that something would happen that would convince us that we're not spinning in a whirlpool headed toward nowhere, but we're floating down the river of eternity guided by God._[9]

1 John 5:6-12 carries a theme of giving testimony to the deity of Jesus Christ. The word _testifies_ or _testimony_ is used nine times and comes from the Greek word signifying someone who has personal and immediate knowledge of something. A Christian's faith is not in a fabricated story or in human theory. Instead, our faith is based on outward and inward evidences given by God.

There are times in all our lives when we doubt our faith and struggle to see God past feelings of grief and loss, a sense of failure, or fear of forces we can't control; we can't reconcile the God of love and justice with some tragedy or obvious evil that attacks us or others. Raymond Edman, former chancellor of Wheaton College, once said, _"You must not doubt in the darkness what God told you when it was light."_ The darkness of our situations can bring doubt and struggle. Obviously things were not different in John's day. Some of the believers he was ministering to seem to be having similar struggles with doubt as he felt the need to address the doubts directly in his letter.

Whenever you or someone else questions the reality of Jesus as Savior, do what John tells the Christians here to do: believe it because God said so! Not only did He say it…He also gave evidence to verify it.

Read 1 John 5:11-12 again. What reality and truth has God clearly testified to so that no one should doubt?

_____

_____

_____

What is the promise to those who believe God?

_____

_____

_____

In verse 12 John makes it very clear that God provides eternal life for us through His Son, Jesus. The following scriptures are often referred to as the Roman Road. They walk you through the steps to receive salvation through Jesus Christ. Mark them in your Bible so you will always be ready to either lead someone to Christ or to simply confirm your hope of eternity. Or, if you have never accepted Christ as your Savior, reading these verses can lead you in the steps to make that a reality in your life. (Refer to The Plan of Salvation, pp 122-123 in the back of this book for more information on how to accept Christ as your Savior.)

The final verse of the Romans Road is verse 12 of this week's lesson. Briefly note what each verse emphasizes.

Romans 3:23–

_____

_____

_____

Romans 6:23–

_____

_____

_____

Romans 5:8–

_____

_____

_____

Romans 10:9-10–

_____

_____

_____

Romans 10:13–

_____

_____

_____

John 5:24–

_____

_____

_____

Acts 16:31–

_____

_____

_____

Ephesians 2:8-9–

_____

_____

_____

1 John 5:12–

_____

_____

_____

Salvation is a way of life John wanted for everyone. He wanted everyone to know the love of Jesus.

In 1 John 5:13 John says he wants everyone that believes to know something. What does he say that he wants every believer to know?

_____

_____

_____

Count how many times the word "know" appears in our text from verse 13 through verse 20. Write down how many you found.

_____

_____

_____

Is there another word that you can think of to use instead of the word "know" to express what John wants you to possess? If so, explain.

_____

_____

_____

_____

Write down what other realities Christians can know for certain, beyond any doubt, with full assurance as stated in the following verses:

1 John 5:14-15–

_____

_____

_____

1 John 5:18-19–

_____

_____

_____

1 John 5:20–

_____

_____

_____

In verses 14 and 15 John makes the statement that we can receive what we ask for in prayer. Most of the time when we read these verses we skip over the words "…if we ask anything ACCORDING TO HIS WILL…." All we see is that God should answer our every prayer if we are a believer. My guess is that each of us has prayed fervently about something, and it did not appear that God answered our prayer. The key is in trusting His will. His answer and our answer probably look much different. Just as we said in Lesson 5, there are some things we will never understand this side of eternity. That is why God is God and we are not. I don't know about you, but I think if I were God I would have made a mess of things by now. I find great assurance in the fact that He knows what He is doing, even if I don't!

After John wrote on the subject of prayer, he went on to write about sin. In verses 16 and 17, according to the *NIV Study Bible*, "the sin that leads to death" was the denial of the deity of Jesus or the failure to believe in Jesus as the Son of God. The false teachers that John kept referring to also led immoral lives and refused to repent of their sin, thus leading to their spiritual death. The rejection of Jesus Christ and the truth of the Word of God is the only sin that truly leads to death. If we sin but then confess it, ask forgiveness, and strive daily to live a life free of sin in obedience to the Word of God, we can still believe in Jesus and have eternal life. This is what John refers to in verses 16 and 17.

In the next few verses of our text, 1 John 5:18-20, John outlines some great truths. Read these verses and list those great truths outlined for us here.

_____

_____

_____

Just when you think John is signing off, he gives Christian believers one last warning in verse 21, which happens to be a reoccurring theme with him. What did he warn them to stay away from?

_____

_____

_____

If you read verse 21 in *The Message* (MSG) it says, "Dear children, be on guard against clever facsimiles." In The New Living Translation (NLT) we find, "Dear children, keep away from anything that might take God's place in your hearts."

What things in the world do you personally have to guard against?

_____

_____

When you became a Christian, what idols did you turn from to worship Jesus?

_____

_____

Is there anything that has taken Jesus' place in your heart? If so, explain. If not, explain how you continue to keep Christ first in your heart.

_____

_____

_____

Deeper Still

Dig for passages about idols in the Old Testament and the New Testament. Find out what types of things were idols and what the consequences were for those who followed idols. This could include warnings against following "other gods." Note the blessings to those who turned from idols to serve the living God.

I think it is interesting to note where John began in 1 John 5. He began with victorious living and ended with a warning to stay true. Even though his thoughts seem to stray from one subject to another, in the end he knew what he wanted to say. You see, nothing will pull you away from victorious living any quicker than allowing something in your life to take the place of Jesus. Giving Jesus the first place in our lives is the secret to victorious living!

In Summary

Now, take some time to go through the text once more (1 John 5).

After studying it a little deeper, write down what you learned from each portion of Scripture. How can you apply what you have learned to your own life?

5:1-5– _____

_____

5:6-12– _____

_____

5:13-15– _____

_____

5:16-17 – _____

_____

5:18-21 – _____

_____

Application

Take some time this week to examine your life. Do you ever allow the enemy to convince you that you are living in defeat? If so, spend some focused time in prayer, asking God Almighty to deliver your thought life from Satan. Ask Jesus to walk beside you, giving you a new resolve to live in victory. Write down your prayer here. Also, write down anything you believe might be taking the place of Jesus in your life. Write down a list of healthy priorities…be sure to make JESUS #1!

_____

_____

_____

_____

_____

Memory Verse

"This is love for _____: to obey His _____. And His

_____ are not _____, (4) for everyone born of God

_____ the world. This is the victory that has _____

the world, even our faith. (5) Who is it that _____ the world?

Only he who _____ that Jesus is the Son of God."

1 John 5:3–5 (NIV)

Notes:

_____

_____

_____

_____

_____

_____

_____

_____

_____

_____

_____

_____

_____

_____

_____

_____

_____

_____

_____

_____

_____

_____

LESSON 8

Read 2 John

Write down your initial thoughts.

_____

_____

_____

Write down any key words you see throughout the text.

_____

_____

_____

John addresses this letter "To the chosen Lady and her children." Some scholars believe that this is referring to an unknown Christian woman in the province of Asia and her children. Yet others believe this is a figurative reference to the local church with the children being the members of that church. Either way, he loves the recipient of this letter just as he loves the recipients of all of his letters.

Don't you just love John's consistency and single-hearted focus? In all of his writings he so earnestly calls people to the two essentials of the Christians life: the truth and the love, which are contained and seen by all in the person of Jesus Christ. In the opening six verses of our text, John uses the words truth and love five times each.

Read 2 John 1-6 again. Write down each time you see the words *truth* or *love* and how these words are interconnected with one another.

_____

_____

_____

Right in the middle of those six verses, in verse 3, John gives a short list of blessings that these Christians and John have been given by God.

Read verse 3. List the blessings God has given them and us.

_____

_____

_____

Do you see these blessings as something that you can someday obtain? Or do you see them as blessings you can enjoy today? Explain.

_____

_____

_____

John has given us so much to learn in these letters about the blessings of the Christian life, the love that Jesus gives us, the love we are to give others, and the truth in the Gospel of Jesus Christ. Truth and love interconnect throughout John's writings.

As you have studied John's writing over the last few weeks, do you think that true love for others and God is possible apart from knowing the truth of Jesus Christ? Explain.

_____

_____

_____

How do the following scriptures connect truth and love?
Psalm 26:3–

_____

_____

_____

Colossians 1:5–

_____

_____

_____

2 Thessalonians 2:10–

_____

_____

_____

1 John 3:18–

_____

_____

_____

2 John 3–

_____

_____

_____

Can you think of an example in your own life or the life of another when attempts to love were not done in truth? Or when someone tried to speak the truth to you or someone acted without using Christ-like love as a foundation? What was the result? (Be sure not to name names. Be careful to protect the hearts of others as you share.)

_____

_____

_____

_____

_____

John's words here remind me of a church in San Francisco that we attended with a young couple while we were visiting California. They picked it because of its popular reputation, never having attended before. It was so packed we had to squeeze into seats in the balcony. There was a lot of happy clapping and arm waving, singing about God's love. The speaker preached, exalting the love of God in every sentence. Yet I started to feel uneasy. Lots of God talk and love talk, yet not one mention of Jesus, Christ, or the Gospel. The God spoken of was an attitude of accepting everyone and everything as if everything were equally good and true. They were celebrating themselves and the world, not a Holy God. I was really troubled by the time we left the church and walked out into the spring sunshine.

"So what did you think of the service? Did you like the church?" I asked the young couple.

"I thought it was great, the best church I ever went to." The young lady answered happily. "You didn't have to believe anything!" she went on to say.

Precisely! How helpful is that, I wondered? Is it really loving to pretend drug addiction and other crippling choices are okay? Is it loving not to offer the only life-giving truth that can deliver people from sin and unite them to God the Father? Since that morning, I have been more aware of self-deceiving and false ways that people in and out of the church speak about love and truth. —**Alice**

The good news of God's love is not just about making people feel good about themselves. Yes, you can build people up and edify them, but part of loving is helping people see when they are turning their backs on God; however, truth and love MUST go hand in hand. When we share truth with someone apart from love, hurt always comes. And sadly, when you love someone but allow them to live in a lie…hurt still comes. Truth and love must go together. John knew this, and he wanted to make sure that the readers of his letters understood. He was leading by example, telling the truth in love ABOUT truth and love!

In verse 6, John gives a simple definition of love. Write that definition in your own words.

_____

_____

_____

Now John is teaching that their love must be informed by truth, and discernment must be utilized. Christians are commanded to act in love toward each other and all people. At the same time, there were people outside and inside the churches that denied the truth about Jesus. John wanted to make sure the believers knew that you can love people without opening yourself up to be controlled or hurt by them.

In verse 7, John gives a definition of a deceiver. Write that definition in your own words.

_____

_____

_____

How could these deceivers be identified? (See also 1 John 2:18-23.)

_____

_____

_____

Read Mark 13:22-23. This is Jesus speaking. Are these warnings only for early Christians. Or do they still apply today? Explain.

_____

_____

_____

What do the following verses have to say about what happens to those who hold on to or follow false teaching?

1 Timothy 4:1-4–

_____

_____

_____

2 Timothy 2:16-19–

_____

_____

_____

2 Peter 2:1-3–

_____

_____

_____

In contrast, what do the following verses have to say about what is promised generally to Christians for hospitality and for good deeds done for Christ?

Matthew 10:41–

_____

_____

_____

Matthew 24:45–47

_____

_____

_____

Mark 9:41–

_____

_____

_____

1 Corinthians 3:10-17–

_____

_____

_____

2 Corinthians 5:9-10–

_____

_____

_____

Look at verse 9 of our main text (2 John), and let's go back to what John's meaning is when talking about deceivers. Verse 9, in particular, speaks of running ahead, which refers to Gnostics who thought they had advanced beyond the teaching of the apostles.

> _I believe we are to trust God for our daily bread and not worry about what we will eat in the future. A great example of this is the Israelites as they were wandering in the desert. God provided manna for them each day, but just enough for that day. If they tried to accumulate too much, in other words store it up, the manna became infested with bugs. Yuck! If you really think about it, we all exhibit a bit of the Gnostic character at times. It's not that we would deny Christ's birth, death, and resurrection, but that we would become too independent and self-reliant. We may_

forget to call upon God for our daily direction and act as though we have our life's circumstances under control. Look around you...does it really seem like our world is "in control?" Are we depending too much on our own strength and not enough on God's strength for our daily living? Are we way ahead of the train? —**Jacki**

This is an important reminder for us daily, as well as a great reminder to be cautious about whom we choose to surround ourselves with. We live in a social society and for some people most of our socializing today happens through media.

Who influences you socially?

_____

_____

_____

In John's day, hospitality and socializing were a big deal. As a matter of fact, we will miss much of the urgency of John's second and third letters if we don't understand the priority of hospitality in New Testament times. Hospitality was not an optional courtesy but a necessity. There were no motels and few options for travelers for overnight lodging and meals. The Jew who was traveling expected to find a Jewish resident in a strange city who would take him in.

When Christ directed his disciples to take nothing for their journey (Mark 6:8), He presumed they could be sure of finding hospitality. Their role was to bring good tidings and God's blessings to their hosts so that hospitality benefitted both the guest and the host. Jesus taught that welcoming a follower for His sake was the equivalent of serving Jesus Himself, and to reject any was to reject Jesus (See Matthew 10:11-14, 10:40; Mark 9:41).

Hospitality played an even greater role as the Christian church movement spread. A missionary like Paul could "go to the ends of the earth" only because he could find hospitality to sustain him in strange cities (See Romans 16:23, Philemon 22). Such provision not only made travel possible for the Apostles and itinerant preachers, but it also fostered a sense of unity among scattered churches. Hearing the teachings of Christ through traveling preachers ministered and built up the scattered body of believers in faith.

Soon hospitality became an expected duty of the local churches, and it was a prerequisite for church leaders (See 1 Timothy 3:2, Titus 1:8). Hospitality was commanded of all Christians, even widows (Romans 12:13, 1 Peter 4:9, Hebrews 13:2, 1 Timothy 5:10). Clear rules regarding hospitality were written down in the Didache, an early church handbook that reveals what issues were faced and dealt with by the early church. For example, no traveling preacher was to stay in a home longer than three days, and no prophet was allowed to ask for money for himself or to solicit from non-Christians.

John was dealing with the problem created by prophets who sought hospitality from Christians but were advocating false ideas about Christ. To provide lodging and food for "deceivers and antichrists," as John labels them, was to support their work and enable them to continue dividing and sabotaging the church (v. 11). John warned the Christians to use discernment when they took in visitors.

Read 2 John 10. When should Christians refuse hospitality to visiting workers, according to John?

_____

_____

_____

How can you show grace to people who deny Christ without endorsing their beliefs and promoting their work?

_____

_____

_____

How can you show hospitality to other true believers?

_____

_____

_____

John gives very practical advice, not only about how to grow in the faith, but also how to protect our faith. He ends this particular letter by telling his readers that he has more to say, but instead of writing it down he will tell them in person when he visits. He finally signs off in verse 13. This verse is said to either refer to the sister of the woman he was writing to OR a sister church of the church he was writing to. Either way, John sets the example in one small sentence that the body of Christ is more than just the local church. We are to stand as the unified body of Christ, supporting each other in truth and love!

In Summary

Now, take some time to go through the text once more (2 John).

After studying it a little deeper, write down what you learned from each portion of Scripture. How can you apply what you have learned to your own life?

1-3– _____

_____

4-6– _____

_____

7-8– _____

_____

9-11– _____

_____

12-13– _____

_____

Application

This week find an opportunity to show hospitality to other believers, your pastor, a missionary, Sunday school teacher, small group leader, or anyone that spends time exalting the name of Christ in your life and the lives of others.

Memory Verse

"This is the _____ in essence: God gave us _____

life; the life is in his Son. (12) So, whoever has the _____ has

life; whoever rejects the _____, rejects life. (13) My purpose

in writing is simply this: that you who _____ in God's Son will

know beyond the shadow of a doubt that you have _____ life,

the _____ and not the _____."

1 John 5:11-13 (MSG)

Notes:

_____

_____

_____

_____

_____

_____

_____

_____

_____

_____

_____

_____

_____

_____

_____

_____

_____

_____

_____

_____

_____

_____

_____

LESSON 9

Read 3 John

Write down your initial thoughts.

_____

_____

_____

Write down any key words you see throughout the text.

_____

_____

_____

This little letter is a great example of the fact that God can use the most common, everyday things to speak truth into our lives. At first glance, this book seems like an insignificant, small letter sent from John to his good friend Gaius. John seems concerned that Diotrephes has ignored good counsel and is causing problems for the church. Again in this letter, hospitality is one of the main topics of conversation. Third John reflects so closely John's call to fellowship and hospitality in his first letter that it is almost as if this letter was saved by the Church to show how practical and essential fellowship really is.

John looks at fellowship and hospitality as evidence of whether church leaders are walking in truth and love or just talking. Today we can learn a lot from John about how to build unity in a congregation or destroy it when Christians do not respect each other's personality differences, viewpoints, and backgrounds. In every letter he wrote, John speaks very fervently of loving each other. He firmly believes in fellowship and hospitality being great soil for friendships to thrive in. John loves the people God has allowed him to minister to, and he has a strong desire to see them grow and thrive in a healthy spiritual environment.

Once again, we get a picture of the soft heart John has for his friends and all those he ministers to as he begins this letter with a very personal greeting, calling Gaius his "dear friend." I love the term "dear friend" don't you?

If John introduced you as his "dear friend," how would that make you feel?

_____

_____

What do you think the qualifications are to be considered a "dear friend"?

_____

_____

How would you feel if someone wrote you a letter like John's to Gaius?

_____

_____

In verse 2, John prays that Gaius' "everyday affairs would prosper." Do you pray like that for your dear friends or does jealousy creep into your thoughts occasionally?

_____

_____

John's words in verse 2 should not be misinterpreted to suggest a promise of prosperity and good health for all believers in this life. It is simply John's personal wish for a friend, just as we may write to our friends.

It is interesting that John goes on to make an analogy between physical health and spiritual well-being. Today the medical community is discovering more and more about the direct relationship between a person's physical health and their mental well-being and attitude. The funny thing is, the Bible has been teaching this idea for centuries. The Bible also teaches that our health is affected by our obedience or disobedience to the Spirit of God.

If your physical state resembled your spiritual condition what would you look like? Would you be vigorous and healthy? Or weak and sickly?

_____

_____

_____

Can you give an example from your life when walking by the truth of God improved your physical and mental health?

_____

_____

_____

Deeper Still

Compare 3 John 3 & 4 with verses 3 & 4 in 1 John. What gives joy to John in both letters?

_____

_____

Compare this to Paul's joy in Philippians 1:3-5.

_____

_____

Have you experienced a similar joy as a Christian? Explain.

_____

_____

Your faith is visible through the joy in your life and the obedience you offer to God the Father. Through that visible faith your reaction to life as it comes at you becomes more and more Christlike every day. John says that offering hospitality to Christian brothers and sisters makes our faith visible.

What are some other ways we can make our faith visible?

_____

_____

_____

John uses the phrase "walking in truth" at the end of verse 4. If our faith is visible in our lives, if Jesus lives in our hearts, if we are walking in the truth, then in return Jesus Christ is visible to all those we come in contact with.

What do YOU think the phrase, "walking in truth" means? (Compare translations)

_____

_____

_____

Read the following scriptures and write down what you learn about "walking in the truth":

Psalm 26:1-3–

_____

_____

_____

Psalm 86:11–

_____

_____

_____

Church leaders should be setting the example of what it looks like to "walk in the truth." If you look at 3 John verses 5 - 8, you get a sense that John has respect for the way Gaius "walked in the truth" by showing hospitality to those within the body of Christ.

Read 3 John 5-8 again and list the ways Gaius built fellowship within the local and scattered body of Christ:

_____

_____

_____

Why was John especially pleased when hospitality was extended to strangers?

_____

_____

_____

What role do you think hospitality plays in the church today?

_____

_____

_____

John saw hospitality to those who were spreading the Gospel of Jesus Christ as a simple way to "walk in the truth" and live out faith in a visible way. Sadly, there are those that have their own agendas and are walking in their own direction. John was dealing with a leader who was walking in a direction that led away from the truth. One of the things that I love about John was that he dealt with issues head-on, but did so out of love and concern for the church. John has to deal with the issues surrounding Diotrephes (3 John 9). Diotrephes is thought to have been a church leader who was dictatorial in his leadership and spoke maliciously of other Christians. He also excommunicated members who showed hospitality to John's messengers.

Read 3 John 9-10. List the ways that Diotrephes was the opposite of Gaius toward visitors, even the Apostle John:

_____

_____

_____

What was Diotrephes' apparent motivation?

_____

_____

_____

Diotrephes seems to be intent on doing things his own way and spreading lies about anyone who opposes him. John strikes another nerve here when he addresses the issue of vicious rumors that are being spread about him and other believers who are choosing to show hospitality to other Christians in need. Basically, Dioptrephes is gossiping. Gossip…that is one ugly word. John intended to deal with the source of rumors (vs 10). John knew that nothing good ever comes out of a rumor mill.

What do the following Scriptures say about gossiping and our tongue? (Keep in mind that our words are the most powerful force in nature.)

Proverbs 11:13–

_____

_____

_____

Proverbs 16:28–

_____

_____

_____

2.Corinthians 12:20–

_____

_____

_____

James 3:1-12–

_____

_____

_____

Proverbs 26:20–

_____

_____

_____

After reading Proverbs 26:20, can you think of a time when you were able to help put out the fire? If so, explain.

_____

_____

_____

Do you struggle with gossiping? _____

Do you need to break the habit of gossiping? If so, list some actions you can begin to take in order to remove the sin of gossiping from your life.

_____

_____

_____

Several years ago I heard a wonderful sermon about the damage caused by gossiping. The pastor offered three specific criteria for repeating something about another person. 1. Is it true? 2. Is it needful? 3. Is it kind? Since that time I heard one more that fits perfectly: 4. Is it your story to tell? The point is: if you can't say "yes" to each of these four questions, then stay silent! —**Jacki**

Gossip is a cancer that eats away, not only at the heart of the person who is being gossiped about, but also at the heart of the one doing the gossiping. Over time it breeds within us a critical spirit that leads us further and further from the truth. John has every intention of dealing with Diotrephes' gossip problem when he arrived, but until he gets there he gives Gaius some advice on how to deal with the Diotrephes situation.

Read 3 John 11. What advice does John give to Gaius as he deals with Diotrephes?

_____

_____

_____

Gaius has quite a bit to deal with. Knowing what his friend was going through, John sent his letter by the hand of Demetrius, who has obviously earned the respect of John and the church. John says in verse 12 that the truth even speaks highly of Demetrius, which basically means that Demetrius VISIBLY lived out his faith and because of that the truth of Jesus Christ was visible. _The Message_ translation indicates that endorsements like the one John gives for Demetrius are not handed out lightly. It reminds us that we usually judge ourselves by our intentions, but others judge us by our actions.

Are you heavy on intentions and light on actions? Explain.

_____

_____

_____

Do you think you would get John's endorsement?

_____

_____

_____

Endorsement or not, John gives us a lot to think about in this short little letter. He hasn't said much, but what he did say certainly packs a punch. Again, this proves that if you REALLY read the word with the expectation of finding life application, you will grow and mature in your walk with Jesus. Maybe you feel like you are far from having the type of walk that would get a "John Endorsement," but I would challenge you to remember that we all have room to grow. Nobody is perfect; however, we must strive every day to do everything within our power to live according to the truth of God's Word. The only endorsement you really need is the endorsement of the Father! Do others see Him in you?

In Summary

Now, take some time to go through the text once more (3 John).

After studying it a little deeper, write down what you learned from each portion of Scripture. How can you apply what you have learned to your own life?

5-8– _____

_____

9-10– _____

_____

11– _____

_____

12– _____

_____

13-14– _____

_____

Application

After studying 3 John, is there any area of your life that you feel like you need to deal with in order to be fully "walking in the truth"? If so, explain.

_____

_____

_____

After answering this question as humbly and honestly as possible, spend some time praying over these issues. Pray over these things every day this next week. Ask God to continually reveal areas in your life where you need growth, and ask Him to raise up within you a "Demetrius heart"! Ask Him to give you the strength to fearlessly "walk in the truth" every single day of your life, being a visible picture of Jesus Christ to a lost and dying world.

Record your prayers below.

_____

_____

_____

_____

_____

_____

_____

_____

_____

_____

_____

Lesson 9

Memory Verse

"And we know that the Son of God has come, and he has given us

_____ so that we can know the _____ God. And

now we live in fellowship with the true God because we live in fellowship

with his Son, Jesus Christ He is the only _____ God, and He is

eternal life. (21) Dear children, keep away from anything that might take

God's _____ in your hearts."

1 John 5:20-21(NLT)

LESSON 10

This Bible Study is meant to cause change in your life. When studying the Word of God it is always important that we leave our "I've got this all to-gether" attitude behind. None of us is perfect, and if we fail to allow God Almighty to challenge us on a daily basis, we run the risk of growing complacent and stagnant in our faith. Our prayer is that you will be able to look back at your time in this study and point to moments of growth in your walk with the Lord. As authors, we were all affected differently by our time spent studying 1, 2, & 3 John. To that end, we have each written a letter in order to give you a glance at the effect these short letters of John had on us.

Your assignment for next week follows our letters.

Over the years, as I have facilitated Bible studies, I always ask the participants how they are going to be different as a result of the study. My heart's desire is that they would be able to enhance the reputation of Jesus Christ because they completed a Bible study. Perhaps it's a new verse, a new truth, or a better perspective…but please let it be something. Attending class, doing the lesson, and walking away unchanged seems very sad to me. So as I began to think about the contents of this closing letter, I went back to the basics. How am I going to be different because I studied 1,2,3 John? What is it that God wants me to "get," to remember, and to put into practice? As I prayed and pondered this question my mind went back to the very beginning, when I first began to learn more about John's motivation for writing these letters.

At the heart of these letters is John's distress over false teachers and false teachings. The basic truth of Jesus Christ and his life, death, and resurrection was being denied. John knew this false teaching was wrong because he had both seen and touched a physical Jesus after His resurrection. This group of heretics would be considered a cult in today's society. In the United States, cult-based religions have more than doubled in the past ten years. What does that mean? We are surrounded by millions of people who do not worship the one true God. And that number is growing at an alarming rate. Just as John was deeply concerned about false teachings, we also need to know what we believe and why we believe it.

None of this surprises God. In fact He must have known the allure of false teachers and false gods because back in the Old Testament he included a warning in the Ten Commandments. Exodus 20:3 - "You shall have no other gods before me." In other words, God demands our total surrender to Him and Him alone.

The overwhelming truth for me from this study is that I (we) cannot afford the luxury of being complacent any longer. We are surrounded by lies, and we must be bold and courageous and speak the truth of God's Word. God calls us to be informed, to know the truth, and to speak the truth. We need to stand firm so that God's truths and principals are not erased from our country and our community. My prayer is that we would stand firm together so that God's name can be enhanced and glorified today, tomorrow, and always. May God continue to bless your Christian walk. **—Jacki**

One of the title ideas we played around with was "Know It. Show It." Not very informative, but it covers what I gathered from this study of John's letters.

The "know it" section is about believing in Jesus because His life, lived for us, was witnessed and verified by Scripture. He is the Son of God. He loves us. I need to know and believe that strongly enough to stand firm when others try to promote false teachings, distracting me from the truth.

I "show it" when I continue to walk with Jesus and when I abide in Him. I want to keep Him by my side, where I can learn through His word and by listening to the Holy Spirit's guidance. I also "show it" when I love others, all others. Not just by serving, but also by showing patience and compassion.

One of the biggest struggles I encounter as a mom is convincing my sons of two foundational truths: 1. I always have their best interest at heart whenever I am guiding them because I want them to be responsible, loving Christian men. All my direction points them in that path. 2. I have experience in many areas that are directly related to their situations, so my credibility is valid. Yet, many times, they go off in a different direction, because they weren't quite won over by my teaching.

John would be nodding his head at this description, and I suppose God might be too. Even with a credible, loving teacher and guide, people like me and like my sons, are tempted to walk away, thinking they've found a short cut, when really they've found a trap.

There is no shortcut to knowing, absorbing, and showing God's teachings. They come from discipline and faith, following what I've been taught and sticking to it. That's what John's letters showed me. **—Erin**

When I read John's first letter, the centuries between us drop away. His caring, fatherly words invite me to experience the same joyful fellowship with Jesus and the Father that he and his fellow apostles did. I can almost hear John saying, "Don't be a stranger, a distant relative: come closer and hang out with us and the Lord."

Like his original readers, we haven't seen Jesus, and no one alive has ever seen God. Can we know for certain what God is like? Can we know for certain that we will live beyond the grave? Is Jesus with us in the evil, suffering, and death that are so much a part of this life? John is eager to clear up any doubts or misunderstanding about God that would keep us from walking with joyful assurance and confident faith as His children.

He wisely starts where Christianity starts: the Incarnation of God in Jesus Christ, fully human and fully God. In John's day, the naysayers and false teachers denied that the Holy God, who is Spirit, would ever take on mortal flesh and become a man. Today it is usually the deity rather than the humanity of Jesus that non-Christians and cults refuse to accept.

To all of these doubters who never knew nor saw Jesus on earth, John declares, "I saw the God of Life, I heard Him, and I touched Him." He witnesses emphatically to the incarnation, death, and resurrection of Jesus Christ as a historical fact, whether or not people know it and believe it. God Himself testified through the Spirit, the water, and the blood. What more could God say about who He is than what He has said to man through sending His Son?

John's vocabulary is simple, but his message is profound. Light, truth, love, life—they are all defined by Jesus Christ and interwoven in Him. Jesus not only embodies these but also illustrates them and imparts them to us by His Spirit. If I want to understand what life truly is and how to love, I must look to Jesus.

John makes it clear that if I really long to enjoy fellowship with God, I have to make choices; I live as close to Him as I desire to, decide to, and discipline myself to live. I love the word "abide" (1 John 2:6); it says more to me than just "walk." Abiding suggests living in Jesus, staying at His side, in order to know where and how he wants me to walk. How I experience life depends on where I see myself at any given moment: whether I am abiding in the world, thinking and reacting to things as if I belong here, or abiding above with Christ.

Am I judging situations and people by what I hear and see or by the truth and love of Christ? Am I comparing myself to others and looking in the mirror of opinion and human approval, or looking in the eyes of Jesus my Lord to see who I am and who I should be like? Am I praying for others and myself according to my desires, or praying to know God's best will and intercede for Jesus to be glorified in their lives and mine?

Do I use the church to serve my interests, like Diotrephes, or do I seek fellowship in unity with one Lord and look for ways to contribute to the strength and faith of others, like Gaius? Do I tithe my time and money to God and give the rest to secular interests, or do I try to surrender everything to Him and serve others 24/7, as Jesus lived for me? Who controls my choices?

A phrase that echoed in my mind throughout this study was "the rest of the story." That was the name of a popular radio program by broadcaster Paul Harvey. He entertained people by revealing some little known background fact about a famous person or event that gave new understanding and significance to something that had happened.

So much happens in this fallen world that is wrong and tragic, so much suffering, violence, and sin. John's teaching reminds me that as humans we can't see the whole story. But we know the rest of the story belongs to the true God of life, and that we live in Him, in Jesus, who came for us. I want to remember His truth and love as I walk toward whatever joys and sorrows lie ahead. I will trust in the God of love who is writing the rest of my story in glory. —**Alice**

1 John 1:5 (MSG) says, "This, in essence, is the message we heard from Christ and are passing on to you: God is light, pure light; there's not a trace of darkness in Him." I think this was the "Aha" moment for me, and it happened just 5 verses into the study. It seems that life these days is full of gray areas—areas where we compromise in one way or another simply because it is easier than fighting. Now, I am not saying that learning to compromise is bad when it comes to certain situations.

What I am saying, is that when it comes to the principles of living set forth in God's Word, I do think that compromising and living in the gray area is a detriment to our very souls. The Word of God says, "There's not a trace of darkness in Him." Ever since studying this portion of Scripture, I have been asking myself, "Is there darkness in me?" We all are fallible and we all are sinners, and I will always battle with the sinful nature of the flesh, so in that aspect the answer to the question is a resounding, "Yes, there is darkness in me." I am, however, looking at that question a bit differently. I have been challenged to examine my thoughts, my actions, and my attitudes daily to see if I have allowed "the darkness" to creep in. Am I living in the gray area? Do I have values that reflect the truth of the Gospel of Jesus Christ? Do I look more like Him or the world?

I truly desire to embrace every day and every moment as an opportunity to experience growth. 1, 2, and 3 John challenged me to take that ongoing growth more seriously. I would love to look more like pure light than darkness in a world that is already dwelling in perpetual night. The only way I can see that happening is to open myself up to the Word of God and allow it to change me from the inside out.

My prayer for you is that you will also allow God's Word to undo you to the point that the only place to go is up! Allow the power of Jesus Christ to make a REAL difference in the way you live your everyday life! Be so much like Christ that everyone who comes in contact with you feels like he or she has been an eyewitness to Jesus Himself! **—Crystal**

Your Assignment

What about you? What has this study meant to you? How is your life different? What have you learned? It is your turn. Write your own letter expressing what you have learned and how you plan to put what you've learned into action. The letters you write will be part of your last class time together. I know you will enjoy hearing what God is doing in the lives of those you have walked this journey with!

"Peace to you, our friends!"

My Letter

_____
_____
_____
_____
_____
_____
_____
_____
_____
_____
_____
_____
_____
_____
_____
_____
_____
_____
_____
_____
_____
_____
_____
_____

PLAN OF SALVATION

As we talked about in Lesson 7, John makes it very clear that God provides eternal life for us through His Son, Jesus. John 5:12 says, "This is the testimony in essence: God gave us eternal life; the life is in his Son. So, whoever has the Son has life; whoever rejects the Son, rejects life." It's important to understand that we do not automatically have the Son and eternal life. As the verse implies having the Son is a deliberate choice, just as rejecting the Son is a deliberate choice.

Our heart's desire is that all of you would spend eternity in heaven with Almighty God. God loves you so much He sacrificed His Son for you. Consider these verses: "For God so loved the world that he gave his one and only Son, that whoever believes in him shall not perish but have eternal life. For God did not send his Son into the world to condemn the world, but to save the world through him" (John 3:16–17, NIV1984).

Eternal life is available to you because you believe. It's as simple as that. God chose to make the plan of salvation simple so that as many as believe would receive the gift of heaven. It's not about what you've done, or who you know, or where you go to church—it's about believing.

Let's review some of the verses from Lesson 7 that are often referred to as the Romans Road. Romans 5:8: "But God demonstrates his own love for us in this: While we were still sinners, Christ died for us" (NIV1984). Think about that…God didn't wait for us to repent and then sacrifice his Son. Jesus died in anticipation of us accepting Him as our Savior.

Romans 10:9–10: "That if you confess with your mouth, "Jesus is Lord," and believe in your heart that God raised him from the dead, you will be saved. For it is with your heart that you believe and are justified, and it is with your mouth that you confess and are saved" (NIV1984). Again, we are reminded that it is our choice to confess, our choice to believe, and our choice to receive. Also the word justified means "just as if I've never sinned." So not only will your sins be forgiven, they will be forgotten. Carry your sinful baggage no more.

Romans 3:23: "For all have sinned and fall short of the glory of God and are justified freely by his grace through the redemption that came by Christ Jesus" (NIV1984). You may be thinking that you don't deserve the glory of heaven because of the sin in your life. As the verse says, "All have sinned." Sin is not unique to you. There is no sin that you have committed that hasn't happened to someone else. We are all sinners. Our sin does not surprise God. Why else would He send His Son to die for us if He didn't recognize our sinful nature? Thinking that you have committed an unforgivable sin is Satan's greatest weapon against you.

For the assurance of heaven, pray this simple prayer. "Today, dear Father, I commit (or recommit) my life to You. I confess that I am a sinner, and I ask You to forgive the sin in my life. I believe that You sent Your Son, Jesus, to this earth as the ultimate sacrifice for my sin. I believe that He died, rose again, and resides with you in heaven. I understand that salvation is a free gift, and I have done nothing to earn it. I want to turn from my sinful life and serve You. Thank You, Father, for loving me and providing a home in eternity for me. Amen."

Name_____

Date_____

We encourage you to tell another Christian of your decision to follow Jesus. Consider asking him or her to be an accountability partner with you. Also, please consider being baptized. It's an outward symbol of shedding your old life of sin and being washed clean by the blood of Jesus. And finally, grow your new faith by attending a Bible-based church and/or Bible study for continued encouragement, guidance, and growth. May God be very real to you, now and in the future.

MEMORY VERSES

Lesson 1

1 John 1:3-4 – We proclaim to you what we have seen and heard, so that you also may have fellowship with us. And our fellowship is with the Father and with his Son, Jesus Christ. We write this to make our joy complete (NIV1984).

Lesson 2

1 John 2:1-2 – My dear children, I write this to you so that you will not sin. But if anybody does sin, we have one who speaks to the Father in our defense— Jesus Christ, the Righteous One. He is the atoning sacrifice for our sins, and not only for ours but also for the sins of the whole world (NIV1984).

Lesson 3

1 John 2:15-17 – Don't love the world's ways. Don't love the world's goods. Love of the world squeezes out love for the Father. Practically everything that goes on in the world—wanting your own way, wanting everything for yourself, wanting to appear important—has nothing to do with the Father. It just isolates you from him. The world and all its wanting, wanting, wanting is on the way out—but whoever does what God wants is set for eternity. (MSG)

Lesson 4

1 John 3:1 – How great is the love the Father has lavished on us, that we should be called children of God! And that is what we are! The reason the world does not know us is that it did not know him. (NIV1984)

Lesson 5

1 John 3:16 —This is how we know what love is: Jesus Christ laid down his life for us. And we ought to lay down our lives for our brothers. (NIV1984) 1 John 3:18 – Dear children, let us not love with words or tongue but with actions and in truth. (NIV1984)

Memory Verses

Lesson 6

1 John 4:2-3 – This is how you can recognize the Spirit of God: Every spirit that acknowledges that Jesus Christ has come in the flesh is from God, but every spirit that does not acknowledge Jesus is not from God. This is the spirit of the antichrist, which you have heard is coming and even now is already in the world. (NIV1984)

Lesson 7

1 John 5:3-5 – This is love for God: to obey his commands. And his commands are not burdensome, for everyone born of God overcomes the world. This is the victory that has overcome the world, even our faith. Who is it that overcomes the world? Only he who believes that Jesus is the Son of God. (NIV1984)

Lesson 8

1 John 5:11-13—This is the testimony in essence: God gave us eternal life; the life is in his Son. So, whoever has the Son, has life; whoever rejects the Son, rejects life. My purpose in writing is simply this: that you who believe in God's Son will know beyond the shadow of a doubt that you have eternal life, the reality and not the illusion. (MSG)

Lesson 9

1 John 5:20-21—And we know that the Son of God has come, and he has given us understanding so that we can know the true God. And now we live in fellowship with the true God because we live in fellowship with his Son, Jesus Christ. He is the only true God, and he is eternal life. Dear children, keep away from anything that might take God's place in your hearts. (NLT)

Memory Verses

BIBLIOGRAPHY

Arthur, Kay, Jill Briscoe, and Carole Mayhall. *Can a Busy Christian Develop Her Spiritual Life?* Bloomington: Bethany House, 1994.

Taylor, Lou, Lisa Harper, Angela Thomas, Joy Williams. *Becoming: The Devotional Bible for Women.* Nashville: Thomas Nelson, 2006.

West, Kim. www.make-my-christian-life-work.com/abide.html

Lucado, Max. *Walking with the Savior.* (Calendar). Grand Rapids: Tyndale, 1993.

Barker, Kenneth, ed. The NIV Study Bible, New International Version. Grand Rapids: Zondervan, 1985.

Bunch, Cindy, ed. The NIV Quiet Time Bible, New Testament & Psalms A Lifeguide Bible. Westmont: InterVarsity Press, 1996.

Wenham, Gordon.J., J. Alec Motyer, Donald A. Carson, and R.T. France, eds. *New Bible Commentary*, 21st Century Edition. Westmont: InterVarsity Press, 1994.

Vine, W.E. *Vine's Expository Dictionary of Old and New Testament Words.* Nashville: Thomas Nelson, 1981.

Warren, Rick. *The Purpose Driven Life.* Grand Rapids: Zondervan, 2002.

RESOURCES

CONCORDANCES

Bible Concordances, (Pocket Series), NKJV, Thomas Nelson Publishers, 1999.

NIV Compact Concordances, Zondervan Publishers, 1993.

Strongest NIV Exhaustive Concordance, Zondervan Publishers, 1989.

DICTIONARIES

Nelson's New Illustrated Bible Dictionary and Concordance, Thomas Nelson Publishers, 1995.

New Bible Dictionary, Second Edition, Inter-Varsity Press, Downers Grove, IL, 1994.

The New Combined Bible Dictionary and Concordance, Baker Book House, 1996. NIV

Compact Dictionary of the Bible, Zondervan Publishers.

VINE'S Concise Dictionary of the Bible, Thomas Nelson Publishers, 2005 (Gives access to Greek and Hebrew words).

COMMENTARIES

Believer's Bible Commentary, Thomas Nelson Publishers, 1989.

Halley's Bible Handbook, Zondervan Publishers, various editions.

New Bible Commentary, 21st Century Edition, Inter-Varsity Press, 1994.

A variety of commentaries are available and useful for single books of The Bible.

ON-LINE RESOURCES

bible.crosswalk.com

biblegateway.com

biblia.com

biblestudytools.com

ewordtoday.com

gotquestions.org

BIBLE READING PLANS

Schedules for reading through the Bible are available at Christian book-stores and sometimes included in a Bible.

Some of the websites listed above under ON-LINE RESOURCES offer various plans and tips for Bible reading.

See Zondervan.com for reading plans that you can customize and print out.

ENDNOTES

1   *The NIV Quiet Time Bible, New Testament & Psalm, A Lifeguide Bible*, (Downers Grove:InterVarsity Press, 1994), 17.

2   Rick Warren, *The Purpose Drive Life*, (Grand Rapids: Zondervan, 2002), 140-141.

3   Kay Arthur, Jill Briscoe, and Carole Mayhall, *Can A Busy Christian Develop Her Spiritual Life?*, (Bloomington: Bethany House, 1994), 186.

4   Max Lucado, *Walking with the Savior*, (Calendar–February 23), (Carol Stream: Tyndale, 1993).

5   *The NIV Study Bible, New International Version*, (Grand Rapids: Zondervan, 1985), 1908

6   Kim West, www.make-my-christian-life-work.com/abide.html.

7   W.E. Vine and Old Testament edited by F.F. Bruce, *Vine's Expository Dictionary of Old and New Testament Words*, (Nashville: Thomas Nelson, 1981), 21, Vol. 3: Lo-Ser.

8   *The NIV Study Bible, New International Version*, (Grand Rapids: Zondervan, 1985), 1910.

9   Max Lucado, *Walking with the Savior*, (Calendar–January 31), (Carol Stream: Tyndale, 1993).

Notes:

_____

_____

_____

_____

_____

_____

_____

_____

_____

_____

_____

_____

_____

_____

_____

_____

_____

_____

_____

_____

Lesson 1

Lesson 2

Lesson 3

Lesson 4

Lesson 5

Lesson 6

Lesson 7

Lesson 8

Lesson 9

Lesson 10

Plan of Salvation

Memory Verses

Biblio-graphy

Resources

CPSIA information can be obtained
at www.ICGtesting.com
Printed in the USA
FFOW04n0758101015